Contents

About the National Council of Teachers of English

The National Council of Teachers of English is dedicated to improving the teaching of English and the language arts at all levels of education. Among its 90,000 members and subscribers are teachers of English language arts, university scholars and educational researchers, school and district administrators, and others concerned about the quality of English language arts teaching and learning in our schools. Members receive their choice of stimulating professional journals, a subscription to *The Council Chronicle* newspaper, discounts on more than 300 books and monographs published or distributed by the Council, and savings on registration fees for educational workshops, conferences, and conventions.

NCTE has written, in collaboration with the International Reading Association, national standards for English language arts learning. NCTE is also involved in efforts to develop meaningful new forms of student assessment through the New Standards Project and in reforming teacher assessment through the National Board for Professional Teaching Standards.

For information on other educational resources relevant to the English language arts, call NCTE Headquarters at 800-369-6283, or learn more by visiting the NCTE Homepage at < http://www.ncte.org >.

Parent's Guide to Literacy for the 21st Century

PRE-K THROUGH GRADE 5

Janie Hydrick

National Council of Teachers of English
1111 W. Kenyon Road, Urbana, Illinois 61801–1096

Manuscript Editor: Hilary Taylor Holbrook

Production Editor: Michelle Sanden Johlas

Cover Design and Interior Design: Pat Mayer

Cover Photograph: Thompson-McClellan Photography

NCTE Stock Number 46880-3050

Library of Congress Cataloging-in-Publication Data
Hydrick, Jane.
    Parent's guide to literacy for the 21st century : pre-K through grade 5 / by Janie Hydrick.
      p. cm.
    "NCTE stock number 46880-3050"—T.p. verso.
    ISBN 0-8141-4688-0 (paper trade)
    1. Language arts (Elementary)—United States. 2. Language arts (Early Childhood)—United States. 3. Education, Elementary—Activity programs—United States. 4. Early childhood education—Activity programs—United States.   I. National Council of Teachers of English. II. Title.
LB1576.H92 1996
372.6—dc20   96-4576

INTRODUCTION

Until quite recently, literacy was generally defined in a very limited way—as the ability to read or write one's own name, for example. A much more ambitious definition of literacy today includes the capacity to accomplish a wide range of reading, writing, and other language tasks associated with everyday life. The National Literacy Act of 1991, for example, defines literacy as "an individual's ability to read, write, and speak in English and compute and solve problems at levels of proficiency necessary to function on the job and in society, to achieve one's goals, and to develop one's knowledge and potential."

Standards for the English Language Arts,
by the National Council of Teachers of English
and the International Reading Association

Evolving definition of literacy

The definition of literacy is constantly evolving to fit the demands of our highly literate, technologically demanding world. In our own lifetime, the definition of literacy has grown from being able to read a book and write a letter to a much broader definition of literacy which includes word processing, the Internet, audiotapes and videotapes, radio and television, analyzing and thinking critically about what we view and hear. In this Information Age that you and I are a part of, we can't possibly keep up with all the information that is available to view and hear, but we can *want* to keep learning, and we can know where to go for *information sources* that will help us keep learning.

Evolving literacy demands on children

Children who can read and write today will not be able to compete in the 21st century with children who are not only competent in the traditional performances of print language, but are skilled in oral language, and are able to respond critically to and perform creatively in multimedia, mass media, and electronic media.

Literate adults in the 21st century are expected to be avid consumers of language not only for recreation and leisure, but also to further their own purposes and gains. Literate adults in the 21st century will control language, not be controlled by it.

It's no longer enough that we, as the 20th-century parents of 21st-century citizens, want our children to become highly literate adults. Our children must be sufficiently motivated themselves to continue to meet the demands of the increasingly highly literate, technologically demanding world that they will live in without us. They must make a personal commitment to lifelong learning.

In 1987, elementary language arts classroom leaders met in Wye Woods, Maryland as part of the English Coalition Conference and drafted a description of the person who might emerge from a language arts-rich classroom in the 21st century. We English Coalition Conference participants were aware of how widely varied each of our own social, personal, and academic experiences had been. We also acknowledged that if we provided opportunities and experiences in today's classrooms which reflected the same assumptions about literacy demands that had governed our own social, personal, and academic experiences, we would be ignoring the demands of a future that are already making a difference in the experiences of today's school children.

Our description of the persons who might emerge from a language arts-rich classroom in the 21st century suggested that they would

- be self-motivated readers and writers.
- use language to understand themselves, others, and the world around them.
- be competent and effective language users and consumers.
- understand the power and purposes of language.
- appreciate and respect other languages and language variations.

This description served as a catalyst for conversations that years later contributed to the writing of national standards for English language arts.

Evolving literacy demands on parents

Not only will the 21st century demand of our children a level of literacy that was certainly not demanded of you and me, the 20th century is already demanding more of us as parents today than it did of our parents in this same century. The scene of sitting with my child on my lap and reading leisurely every evening alternates with the scenes of soccer practice, music lessons, and homework with which I can help less and less confidently as my children move up in the grades. Further, with the media's overwhelming emphasis on leisure and recreation, we parents have an increasingly difficult time engaging our children in what we think of as literacy activities.

Evolving literacy in schools

Schools are responding to the increased literacy demands in a variety of ways. The effect of those responses on us as parents can be confusing and often overwhelming and discouraging. Parents have lots of questions about how schools are changing curriculum and expectations to meet these increased literacy demands, but we're often not sure where to go with our questions.

You've probably asked at least one of these questions:

- What's going on in my child's school? I have a calendar of school events, but what's going on in the classroom and why?
- What do all these new or recycled terms mean? Are things really different from when I was in school?
- How can I help my child and not go against what the school is doing?

- Is what I'm doing with my child the right way or the wrong way to do it?
- How can I help my child prepare for the 21st century without giving up my job so I can have the time to do it?

This book is designed to answer all those questions and more.

Perspectives of a parent, teacher, and professional leader

I wanted very much to write this book because I have three different, but complementary, perspectives on preparing our children for literacy in the 21st century. The first perspective is that of a parent, the second is that of a 30-year classroom teacher, and the third, that of a past president of the National Council of Teachers of English.

As a parent, I have experienced the same confusion that non-teaching parents experience when they try to make sense of what their children are doing in school. The specific curriculum and activities that go on in my children's classrooms are not exactly what goes on in my own classroom. There are some basic concepts that all of the classrooms have in common, though, and if I focus on the commonalities, then the differences seem less crucial and more a question of an individual teacher's methods. The differences contribute less to a sense of confusion than to a rich diversity of educational opportunity and experience.

As a teacher, I have seen many changes in curriculum and expectations. The curriculum, materials, and the way I teach today are in many ways different from the curriculum, materials, and the way I taught 30 years ago. But there are basic concepts that have prevailed, as well as a basic belief in kids and in their capacity for learning. Parents today, just like their counterparts 30 years ago, want their children to succeed in school and in life. Parents today, just like their counterparts 30 years ago, want to play a part in helping to make their children successful, but they're not sure what they should do, and are often afraid that they might do the wrong thing.

As a past president of the National Council of Teachers of English, I've had the opportunity for almost five years to be current with trends and issues in education, particularly with English studies and language arts. I've been able to cultivate a national perspective as well as keep abreast of developments on the state and local level.

The composite perspective I offer to you in this book, then, is that of a parent with 30 years of classroom experience and with experience on a national level. It's a composite of perspectives which work together to help me understand what your concerns are, and what you can do with your children's teachers and at home to prepare your children for the literacy demands of the 21st century.

How the book is set up

This book is divided into five sections as follows:

Basics
>   basic skills
>   cooperative learning
>   authentic assessment
>   multiage grouping
>   multiculturalism

Language
>   oral language
>   dramatic play
>   grammar and usage
>   language acquisition
>   bilingual education
>   ESL (English as a Second Language)

Reading
>   emergent literacy
>   environmental print
>   trade books
>   pattern books and predictable books
>   literature-based reading programs
>   response to literature
>   media literacy

Writing
>   writing workshop
>   freewriting
>   process writing
>   invented spelling
>   poetry

Across the Disciplines
> literature across disciplines
> integrated language arts
> thematic units
> family literacy

These five sections don't represent any particular way that class-rooms or curriculum are, or should be, divided. They were simply a convenient way to cluster terms and concepts that are addressed in this book. Let me illustrate with an analogy. Think of the five sections as five separate ponds of water. As a reader, you can physically access the book sections in the same way that you can step into the separate ponds, by simply dipping into any one of the separate sections you wish. Concep-tually, however, the book is more like a stream. Some water may reside at any particular moment in a pool, among the rocks, lap at the banks, or even be trapped in separate ponds. The water is always, however, part of the stream. In a similar way, a language arts concept (oral language, media literacy, or thematic units, for example) may reside at any particular moment in the pool, bank, or pond formed by the section on language or reading or across the disciplines. The concept is always, however, part of the whole stream of language arts.

As you read the different sections of the book, I hope you will transcend the categories that convenience placed on the organization of this book, that you will go beyond dipping into separate ponds, and that you will understand the power of a stream that has so many different waters contributing their separate yet overlapping strengths to a single flow.

Each section will have

- an *introduction* to the concepts included in that section and an explanation of why those concepts were clustered together.
- a *definition* of each concept.
- a *vignette* to illustrate what each concept might look like in a school or home setting.
- *activities* for home that support each concept.

All of the vignettes are based on my own experiences as a parent and classroom teacher. Although each vignette is specific in that it serves to illustrate a particular grade level or concept, each vignette is also generic in that it can easily represent a wide range of learners and learning situations.

The lists of suggested activities are short, not exhaustive, and are designed only as a springboard for your own ideas. Not all of the activities may be appropriate for you and your children. Begin with an activity you can do easily and comfortably with your children. Then add to the list those activities that work especially for you and your children.

How should this book be read? It's not a novel that must be read from beginning to end. However, the heroes and heroines can be you and your children as well as the characters you find in books; and the settings can be your choice: a rocking chair, the dining room table, the car, or a cozy corner. Open the book to a section you are most comfortable with, or most interested in, and let the literacy adventure begin!

BASICS

This section entitled **basics** includes ways that teachers have of structuring the class, and ways of conducting the children's learning and assessment. All of these ways are very important lenses through which we all can see kids and learning.

There are as many definitions of **basic skills** as there are people who give basic skills any thought. A list of basic skills can include anything from sounding individual letters to problem solving. The skills you include in your own list of basic skills depend on what you consider *basic* or *fundamental* for survival in this highly literate world of ours. A teacher's list of basic skills is the lens through which the teacher sees what is basic or fundamental in each day's activities.

Authentic assessment is a way of looking at the way we test or assess the important things we teach, not just what we call the basic skills, but anything else we think is important to assess. The time that is spent on assessment in each classroom, and the form that the assessment takes will determine how the children's time and energy are spent.

Multiage grouping is a lens through which schools can determine who the student population will be in the classroom, and it allows for placing children in a broader age range than is possible in a single grade level. Although a typical fifth-grade classroom, for example, may have children within a two-year age range, from ten to twelve years old, a multiage classroom may have children within a five-year age range.

Cooperative learning is a lens through which we see and value how the children work together. Cooperative learning is not simply a way of grouping children or assigning tasks. It is an acknowledgement that each child in the classroom can be a source of help and information to every other child in the classroom.

Multicultural issues help us evaluate and select what material is used in the classroom, and how that material is presented.

So, the way schools view basic skills, authentic assessment, cooperative learning, multiage grouping, and multicultural issues determines not only who is in the classroom, but what is taught, how it is taught, and how it is assessed. These are all classroom basics.

Basic Skills

There is no single, definitive list of basic skills. Through the years, and until the late 20th century with its unprecedented proliferation of information and technology, the term "basic skills" had come to mean those skills which a person must have to survive and on which to build other skills. In other words, a person who could read and write independently didn't need to work on basic skills.

There are as many lists of basic skills as there are people interested enough in composing such a list. The criteria used for defining those basic skills are contingent upon how specifically the skills are defined and upon one's definition of basic.

One hundred years ago, basic skills might have included being able to read some common signs, read a few passages from the Bible, write a list of groceries or chores, and write a short message or letter. The writing skills would not have included stringent criteria about spelling because at that time there were still many acceptable variations in spelling even common words.

When I was a middle-grade student in the 1950s, basic skills included being able to read a story or novel independently, write a short report, score well on weekly spelling tests and tests on grammar and usage, and give an oral book report. Those of us who finished our work early could dabble in creative writing, but that certainly wasn't a basic skill expected of everyone.

Today's world calls for a much higher level of "basic." Today, basic skills probably include reading a mass transit schedule, filling out a tax form, writing a letter, reading a wide variety of manuals (for example, small appliance or toy assembly instructions, electronic game directions, software documentation), and a level of critical thinking that protects us from being completely manipulated by commercial advertising, political advertising, and editorial bias. Today's basic skills also include the skills of organizing one's work and of working together with others. As you can see from this partial listing, basic skills are no longer confined to survival in printed matter. We must survive today in what we encounter through radio, television, film, and computer.

Not only does today's world call for a much higher level of "basic," but we have become more specific about what we want to mean by "skill." At one time, "reading" was listed as a basic skill, and educators and other decision makers were allowed a wide range of interpretations of what "reading" might mean and how it might be taught and supported. Today, "reading" has been broken down for some into a long laundry list of specific skills that includes initial consonants, digraphs, fluency, diphthongs, and so on. This specific-skill view of "reading" has dramatically altered how "reading" is regarded and defined as well as how it is taught and supported.

Any list of basic skills that you make should include all the skills that you can imagine your children will need to have not only to survive but to do well in the 21st century. You should look at your list of skills not simply as an instructional or achievement goal, but as a foundation that your children will want to continue building upon for lifelong learning and lifelong success.

What can basic skills look like?

Lilia walks into the kitchen where Jesse is fixing dinner. "Dad," she says, "I have to watch the news tonight. We're doing this thing on campaign ads. When is it on?" He rolls his eyes. "So what am I, a

walking *TV Guide?* There's the paper. Find out for yourself." With a little
help, Lilia finds the time and channel for the local newscast. The
program doesn't air for another 15 minutes, so she pulls out her
homework sheet and looks at the questions she and her classmates put
together that day in class. The questions include "Would the ad make
me vote for the candidate? Why?" "What words in the ad were sup-
posed to persuade me?" "What was the candidate doing in the ad?"
"Who were the other people in the ad and what were they doing?" "Did
the candidate just talk about himself or herself or did the ad blast the
opponent?" Then Lilia has an idea. "Dad, should I tape the ads? Then
everyone in my group could look at the same ads over and over tomorrow and really pick them apart." The father answers, "If you want
several to look at, then why don't you set the timer on the VCR and tape
the news tonight after you've gone to bed? The VCR manual's right
there on the TV. Go for it!"

Alyson McDuffy, age 7

What can we do at home?

✎   Make a list of skills you use every day. Make sure the list includes academic skills, for example, reading, writing, math; social skills—being cooperative, supportive; work skills— organization; and thinking skills—being critical, analytical. You might want to break down some of the larger skills into smaller ones. After you've made the list of skills you use every day, make a list of skills that you think your children will need to have when they are adults. How do the two lists compare?

✎   Ask your children's teachers for a curriculum overview. What skills are being emphasized with each child? Which are not? How does the school list compare with the lists you made? Does the school list cover academic, social, work, and thinking skills? You could schedule a conference with your children's teachers to discuss the three lists of skills. Remember, too, that there is a lot that goes on in a classroom that is not reflected in a curriculum overview, particularly the social, work, and thinking skills, and schools do not assess those skills in the same way that they assess skills that are traditionally included in a curriculum overview.

✎   Obtain standards from subject-matter organizations such as the National Council of Teachers of English and the National Council of Teachers of Mathematics. These standards include skills that members feel our children will need in the 21st century. Many of those standards are available by calling the organization or by going to your local public library, college or university library.

This list of suggested activites is short, and is designed only as a springboard for your own ideas. Begin with an activity you can do easily and comfortably with your children. Then add those activities that work especially well for you and your children.

Cooperative Learning

In most classrooms, children will sometimes work competitively, sometimes work individually and alone, and sometimes work cooperatively. The tasks and the goals or rewards combine to determine how the children will work. For example, if the children are engaged in a contest or if they know that there will be a limited number of high scores for a task, then they will work competitively and not work to help each other. If a child is working on a task that no other child is working on, then the child will work individually and alone. When children are aware of the potential of others to help, and when the task and classroom environment encourage their working together, then the children will work cooperatively.

The term cooperative learning can refer to a wide range of classroom practices that involve children working with other children. Although two or more children working together may be learning cooperatively, the term cooperative learning usually refers to a structured model or at least to a set of specific characteristics for small-group activity.

In cooperative learning, acquiring skills of working together is just as important as the academic skills and information that come from working together. Children develop their skills in listening to each other, encouraging each other to participate in the group setting, and contributing ideas for the good of the group. They learn that, if all members of the cooperative learning group participate as they should, it is true that "Two heads are better than one."

What can cooperative learning look like?

The third graders have divided themselves into groups to study Native Americans. The group studying the Haida has four children in it. Devon organizes the group by giving Melissa and Shanna pieces of blank paper. "Melissa," he says, "put a big K at the top of your page and we can put down everything we already know about Haida." "Oh, I know," says Shanna, "my paper will have a W, all the things we want to learn about." All four of the group members call out items eagerly to be placed on the two lists, and occasionally you can hear comments like

"Yeah, that's a good one," or "Neat," or "Uh huh, that's okay." When Brad responds to an item with "You mean you don't know that, Shanna?" the others in the group remind him that he wasn't being encouraging.

What can we do at home?

✎ Share with your children the ways you use cooperative learning at work. How do you and the other workers support each other in your work? When and how do you and other workers work together toward a special goal?

✎ Sit down with your children and make a list of tasks that are done around the home. Which tasks are done competitively, individually, or cooperatively? Can any of the tasks be done better if you work differently?

✎ Think of tasks around the home that can be done cooperatively and have the children help create a cooperative group to get the task done. For example, if the car needs to be cleaned, make a list of the separate tasks that need to be done (wash windows, wash tires, wash car body, vacuum inside, clean mats, empty out litter, etc.). What materials are needed to clean the car? What individual tasks can each family member do to clean the car? Before starting to clean the car, discuss ways that family members can be supportive of each other. After the car is cleaned, talk about how important each family member's task was and how you all encouraged each other during the cleaning.

✎ Sit down with your children and discuss what they did in school that day. Did they work competitively, individually, or cooperatively? Could the work have been accomplished better if they had worked differently?

This list of suggested activites is short, and is designed only as a springboard for your own ideas. Begin with an activity you can do easily and comfortably with your children. Then add those activities that work especially well for you and your children.

Authentic Assessment

A uthentic assessment is evaluation that is in agreement with experience. In language arts, assessment has to take into account not only how children use language to accomplish a particular purpose, but what they know about language in terms of rules and usage. It's easiest to begin by looking at some traditional methods of assessing language arts to see what it is that these methods cannot assess. If I give my fifth graders a test with ten sentences and ask them to identify the usage error in each one (for example, "I can't have *no* friends over to play."), I am assessing their ability to identify usage errors. I am not, however, assessing their ability to apply correctness of usage in speech or writing in a variety of situations or contexts. I am not assessing their ability to communicate ideas or their ability to adjust writing format for purpose or audience.

Authentic assessment, then, can include many procedures and objects such as teacher observation and recording in the form of anecdotes or logs; student self-observation and recording; photographs, audiotapes, and videotapes; collections or portfolios with a wide range of student work. Each of those procedures and objects can be analyzed and summarized separately or as a composite profile of the child.

Authentic assessment tied to the particular class activity described in the following vignette included letters, photographs, and sample petitions students placed in their portfolios that reflected their communication of ideas; anecdotes which we recorded about their language decisions (format, correctness, audience) and language consciousness (situation and context); and student reflections about how their active participation in a democracy was made possible through their effective use of language.

Authentic assessment is more complex than traditional assessment forms are, but it is a more satisfactory and comprehensive way to assess the complex aspects of language use.

What can authentic assessment look like?

The fifth graders were concerned with the effect of toxins such as HCFCs on the atmosphere, and decided to inform people about the dangers of HCFCs and to raise the level of concern in as many people as possible. After exploring the possibilities for reaching the most people with their message, the students decided to circulate petitions and to write letters to the local newspaper and their United States senators. In writing their petitions and letters, they realized that correctness and presentation would be very important, so they took great care with usage and spelling, and they used the laser printer for their final copies. They planned their strategies for gathering petition signatures, and contacted local grocery store managers for permission to schedule tables in front of the stores. They sent cover letters and petitions to every elementary, junior high, and secondary school in their large school district. Several of their letters to the editor of the local newspaper were published, and the students mailed to their two senators a package of over 8,000 signatures on petitions. In return, the students received letters and pictures from the senators and from then-President Bush. In her portfolio, Nikki placed a copy of the newspaper in which her letter to the editor was published, a videotape of herself at the petition table she set up in front of a local grocery store, and a copy of the action log her working group of five classmates had kept. Nikki's teacher added to the portfolio two anecdotes that she had written about Nikki: one about Nikki's leadership in contacting grocery store managers and scheduling classmates to gather petition signatures, and one about Nikki's writing conference with the teacher to refine the letter to the editor.

What can we do at home?

     Begin a portfolio for each of your children. Put at least one item in the portfolio each week. These portfolio items could include a note written to a parent, a chore list, a great paper from school, a photograph of a play the children put on for you, a poem, an audiotape of a readaloud, or a videotape. Attach a small piece of paper to each portfolio item that gives a little background for the item (name of child, date, why the item was selected to put in the portfolio). Birthdays and New Year's Eve are great times to look at all the portfolio items.

     Keep a portfolio of your work and share the portfolio items with your children. These items could include notes or evaluations from your supervisor, things that you have made or written at work, awards, or certificates for advanced training.

✎ Ask your children's teachers what sorts of assessments they use in the classroom. Do they use combinations of assessments? Are the assessments daily? weekly? monthly? Are they fill-in-the-blank? multiple choice? essay tests? Do the teachers observe the children and record anecdotes? Do the children keep portfolios? Are the children part of the assessment process?

✎ Ask how your children are assessed in non-academic classes such as P.E., music, and art. Do your children understand those assessments?

✎ Find out how your children are assessed in after-school sports and music lessons. Do your children understand those assessments?

This list of suggested activites is short, and is designed only as a springboard for your own ideas. Begin with an activity you can do easily and comfortably with your children. Then add those activities that work especially well for you and your children.

Multiage Grouping

Multiage grouping is not a new concept. Multiage grouping is a way schools assign children to a particular classroom that allows for a broader range of ages in one classroom than does grouping by single age or grade level.

There are many variations in applying multiage grouping. The multiage groups may function as groups for one or more parts of the school day, or for the entire school day. The grouping can be school wide and representative of the entire school population, or can be limited to a narrower population such as primary and intermediate.

Multiage grouping provides opportunities for children to interact regularly with other children of many ages, abilities, interests, and backgrounds. Curriculum and work groups must be flexible enough to correspond to the children's individual abilities, needs, interests, and backgrounds.

Multiage grouping requires a wide variety of learning opportunities and instructional strategies, and the children's engagement with methods of inquiry and their understanding of major curricular concepts have more importance than do narrow, specific skills or short-term goals.

Multiage grouping resembles life outside of school: groups representing many ages and many abilities working together on problems, issues, and concepts that hold the interest and respond to the needs of people with very different backgrounds.

What can multiage grouping look like?

Five children are clustered around a rabbit cage: Toby (11 years old), Letisha (9 years old), Sami (6 years old), and the twins, Amanda and Alonzo (8 years old). They've been working for several weeks on a study of rabbits and are planning how to share their findings with the rest of the class. The study began after spring break when Letisha brought in a rabbit her grandfather had given her. Toby called it a "dumb bunny," but Sami hopped to the rabbit's defense by saying that rabbits were used a lot in science experiments, so they couldn't be dumb. The discussion that followed involved several other children, including Amanda and Alonzo, and the children were fascinated enough by the questions they raised during the discussion to form a study group to find some answers. Sami was determined to prove once and for all that the rabbit was not a "dumb bunny." Toby used his past experience in behavioral science to guide Sami in setting up some maze training. Studying—and playing with—the class's two gerbils, three hamsters, rat, and tortoise had provided Toby with the basics he needed to help build a maze as well as design a set of runs and a system of recording and charting the rabbit's progress. Amanda and Alonzo were intrigued by multiple births and genetics. Letisha needed to find out more about how to care for rabbits.

What can we do at home?

✎ Ask your children's teachers about the opportunities your children have to work in multiage groups. Do your children have a regularly scheduled time for activities involving reading buddies or pen pals from different age groups, for example?

✎ Talk with your children about your situation at work. Make a list of the people you work with from different age groups. Talk about how you work together.

✎ Provide opportunities for your children to work in multiage groups. When fifth graders, preschoolers, and grand-parents work together on interests, problems, and projects, they all benefit.

✎ Sit together as a family and plan your family activities around a common interest or issue that provides every member the opportunity to have a special role. For example, if the family wants a dog, you can all sit down and make a list of issues that the family must address before buying a dog. (Where will we buy it? From a pet shop, dog pound, friend? What kind should we buy? How do we train it? How do we take care of it and who will do it?) Each of those questions and more need to be answered and agreed upon before a family can successfully buy and care for a dog.

✎ Multigenerational grouping is a grand extension of multiage grouping. Your children, regardless of age, could visit retired people in their homes or in nursing homes and just talk, sharing stories and good times. They could read to each other. The children could make cards for them or teach them to play

games or finger plays. They could sing, play the piano, or
dance for each other. They could draw, visit a museum, find
constellations, or cook together.

*This list of suggested activites is short, and is designed only as a springboard for your
own ideas. Begin with an activity you can do easily and comfortably with your
children. Then add those activities that work especially well for you and your children.*

Multiculturalism

Multiculturalism is another term that has different meanings for
different people. Generally, culture means the way a group lives,
and it can include the way that the group acts, what the group believes
and values, and what the group creates. The group that is represented
by a culture can be one that sets itself apart because of ethnicity,
geographic origin, gender, or some other attribute.

In classrooms, multiculturalism can be seen as a way of valuing
multiple groups. A study of American history in fifth grade would
include the contributions of the first Americans who crossed Beringia;
the Aztec, Maya, and Inca civilizations; the North American Indians; and
all of the other cultures that continue to contribute to the rich diversity
of our nation.

Multiculturalism does more than value the contributions of multiple
groups to the development of a single nation, it values the separate and
unique differences each culture represents. For example, Navajo culture
is valued—and taught—in part because of the contributions of Navajos
to the development of our nation, from pre-Columbian art, to World
War II code talking, to contemporary nuclear science. Navajo culture is
also valued and taught because there are aspects of the Navajo culture
that are very different from aspects of any other culture in our country.
To privilege any culture exclusively for study of its history and contributions would be to ignore much of our nation's history, as well as the
contributions and backgrounds of many of our people, past and
present.

We used to refer to our country as a melting pot of many cultures.
Food analogies work well for me. There is a delightful stew in our

melting pot, with a tantalizing, mouth-watering smell that can only be described as "stew." When you take a spoonful of that delectable dish, you are tasting "stew," yet with very little effort, you can make out the individual, distinct flavors of the vegetables. Each vegetable makes a unique contribution of taste and texture to that heavenly concoction. With the omission of any single vegetable, the stew would be different, yet with the addition of all the vegetables, it is the greatest stew in the world.

What can multiculturalism look like?

The children had been studying Native American tribes of Arizona for two weeks. Tony's father was an Apache, so the children wrote him a letter, inviting him to come in to talk to them about his culture. They set up a day and time, and cleared the project with the media specialist. Tony shared with his classmates ahead of time the list of artifacts his father would be bringing in. The third graders were very excited because they had seen pictures and small models of many of the real artifacts they would soon be seeing and touching. Tony's father arrived early and surrounded the presentation area with cradle boards, drums, flutes, bows, arrows, baskets, and many other pieces, each one with a story, each one representing an important part of Apache life—an important part of Tony's life.

What can we do at home?

✎   Trace your own family's history and cultural background. How many groups are represented?

✎   Make a list of traditions that your family keeps. Can you trace the cultural origins of those traditions? How about food, favorite stories or books, music, clothing?

✎   Take the list of your own family traditions and compare them with traditions of other families and other cultures. What are the similarities? What are the differences?

✎　Take one item and trace it through other cultures. For example, take egg rolls from China, spring rolls from Laos, lumpia from Indonesia, burros from Mexico, pierogies from Poland. How and why are they alike or different?

✎　Make a list of foods, traditions, literature, music, clothing, etc. that you think of as being American. Can you trace the cultural origins of each one?

This list of suggested activites is short, and is designed only as a springboard for your own ideas. Begin with an activity you can do easily and comfortably with your children. Then add those activities that work especially well for you and your children.

LANGUAGE

In this section, I will present several topics which generally come to mind when people talk about language: the communication of meaning through words.

We think of **language acquisition** with infants as coming about through **oral language**. That is, our children first learn our language by listening to us talk to them, sing to them, and read bedtime stories to them. Through their many and varied experiences in oral and written language, children also acquire a sense of **grammar and usage**, and they become aware of a need for correctness in grammar and usage.

Dramatic play allows children of any age to experiment with the language of many other roles and situations. Dramatic play also provides children with a low- or no-risk environment in which to express their own feelings.

Finally, **bilingual education** and **ESL** (English as a second language) education provide opportunities for children to expand the expressions and understandings they have through their first language by learning a new language.

Oral Language

Anyone who has been around children knows how important oral language is to children. They're always talking and listening to each other. When we adults come together, we also talk and listen to each other. Some of us even talk to ourselves! Oral language can be taught apart from the other language arts and seen as a set of discrete, separate skills. Oral language can also be supported consciously in classrooms by making it a purposeful, assessed part of the language arts curriculum. Oral language can also be supported as a vital component of learning in all disciplines. Or oral language can be assumed and, subsequently, ignored or neglected.

Aspects of oral language in the classroom include timing (when it is particularly encouraged), purpose (what children need to gain from it), form (group discussion, individual presentation, etc.), specificity of skill (level of formality, awareness of audience, eye contact, etc.), and context (literature response, math, etc.).

Children's talking is important because it is a natural way for them to verbalize or to express what they know and what they are learning. Bring a rabbit into a kindergarten class and you'll hear the children talk about everything from the tortoise and the hare, to Peter Rabbit, to commercials with rabbits, to Easter, to pet care, to the petting zoo, to the state fair. Children of any age can present what they know to small or large audiences. Preschoolers can show their classmates a new toy and share how each little piece works. A fifth grader can demonstrate to several classmates how to blend paints on a palette.

Children's talking is also a natural way for them to test out new ideas and theories about their world and their learning experiences. Second graders learning about planets will hold lively discussions about what they know, what they're learning, a trip to the local planetarium, stars they've seen at night, and the possibilities of life on another planet.

Finally, children's talking is an important way in which they can express and share connections between new information and comfortable ways of thinking. When firefighters come into our elementary schools to talk about fire safety, there's always time after the presentation for questions. Questions in the primary grades are not necessarily in the form of questions, but in the form of shared experiences or shared stories. Nate will tell about a fire he saw in a movie. Jeanna's uncle was in a fire and his house burned down. Dorie's mother burned a hole in the couch with her cigarette. The children are making connections between information the firefighter has presented and the experiences and knowledge the children already have.

Teachers are particularly supportive of oral language in the class-room when they provide an atmosphere in which children are encouraged to talk and in which children understand the value of their talking. Teachers can model attentive listening, and they can help the flow of oral language in the classroom by discussing aspects such as taking turns, not interrupting, responding thoughtfully, and asking pertinent and appropriate questions.

Teachers can involve the children in assessing their own oral language in the classroom by having them list ways and contexts in which oral language is effective (starting and maintaining conversations, speaking clearly, using appropriate volume, explaining division of fractions, telling a story). Teachers can also involve the children in determining ways that the assessment of oral language can be made (oral or written responses, anecdotal records, checklists, etc.).

Oral language is vital to learning. It must be valued and have a clear place in classroom learning as well as home experience.

What can oral language look like?

Nancy and her preschooler are stopped at a red light. "Did you play with anyone special today?" asks Nancy. "Yeah," Jamie answers. "Tell me about it." "Well, Richie and me played in the sandbox." The light changes and Nancy accelerates. Jamie is silent. "What did you play, Jamie?" "Stuff," he answers. Nancy continues. "Did I ever tell you about the time I got lost in the sandbox and Grandmom couldn't find me for three weeks? Or the time my friend Tina and I dug all the way down to China?" Jamie giggles. "Can Richie come over and play, Mom? We had this really neat idea for making a tunnel in the sand." "I guess," says Nancy. "You can call him right after we get home from shopping." "Can we get popsicles at the store?" asks Jamie. "We'll eat them outside in the sandbox. We won't mess. Then we can use the sticks in our tunnel."

What can we do at home?

✎　Talk to your children and let them talk to you. Be active listeners for each other. Ask them today about something they told you yesterday.

✎　Use the tape recorder or video camera to record your children giving directions on how to play a game or how to make a peanut butter-and-jelly sandwich.

✎　Ask your children to tell you about one thing that happened during the day (at school or at home). Encourage them to tell you lots of interesting details about a short period of time or about a single event, rather than a general list that represents an entire day. This is a good activity to do in the car.

✎　When several family members are gathered together, ask one child to tell about a story you've been reading together, or about the trip to the grocery store, or about a pretty car you saw while driving.

✎　Pretend you are a robot. Ask your child to give you specific directions on how to spread peanut butter on a cracker (including getting all materials together), how to sweep the floor, how to mix a glass of chocolate milk, or how to give a hug. Follow your child's directions exactly!

✎　Arrange to have your children interview a friend or relative. Interviewing grandparents can be lots of fun. Have your children make a list of questions beforehand. The interviews can be shared orally, and later can be written up and made into a short book.

✎　When you are shopping, have your children ask for directions to a particular section of the store. Then have your children repeat the directions to you and lead you to that section.

Younger children love making announcements. Ask them to announce that dinner is ready (encourage them to improvise and add humor, additional information, etc.), that you are going to the store, that a special television or radio program is coming on, that someone in the family has accomplished something special, that it's instrument practice time, or that it's time for a family hug.

The next time an older child wants to do something, have the child prepare a speech of persuasion. The speech can be prepared simply by having the child list reasons in favor of being able to do it and then presenting the list orally.

With older children, have them take an opposing point of view and debate it with you. It can be a topic in which the child has no vested opinion, a topic about which the child feels strongly and must take the opposite point of view in this debate, or a topic about which the child feels strongly and is allowed to debate from that point of view. Should children clean their own rooms and if so, how often? Should children eat everything on their plates? Should children have chores? Should children be limited in television viewing?

Read aloud to your children. Books as well as poems can provide a rich array of vocabulary, sentence structure, simile, alliteration, and detail, for example.

Select poems or short passages from books that contain special uses of language for you and your children to memorize and recite. Some of the language use will linger and pop up in the children's talk.

Cut out pictures from magazines or the newspaper and have your children describe the picture or tell a story to accompany the picture. Use old family photographs and have your children weave different stories or more elaborate stories.

This list of suggested activities is short, and is designed only as a springboard for your own ideas. Begin with an activity you can do easily and comfortably with your children. Then add those activities that work especially well for you and your children.

Dramatic Play

D ramatic play can be used in many different ways in the home and the classroom. Children can place themselves in the roles of characters as varied as a working father or a princess; they can demonstrate their understanding of a story through the dramatization of a scene; they can respond to an event or a book through a dramatization; they can act out scenes or try on characters they might want to use in their writing; or they can express their own feelings safely within the context of being a different character. This, of course, is only a short list of possibilities.

What can dramatic play look like?

"Sit down and eat your peas," orders Andrew, "I'll cook your steak and have it for you in a jiffy." "Mmmmmmm, that smells good. Where's my paper?" asks Amina, tottering in her size 7, three-inch high heeled shoes. "Over there," says Andrew, pointing, "Don't forget to read to the baby." Amina picks up the baby and the newspaper. "Once upon a time in Phoenix, there was a car that crashed into a tree. 'Oh no,' said the policeman. 'There's broken car all over. I better call the ambliance.' " Andrew walks over from the wooden sink to the table. "Here's your steak. Oops, it fell on the floor." He leans over to pick it up. "That's okay, dear," comforts Amina, dropping both the baby and the newspaper as she totters over to help Andrew pick up the steak.

What can we do at home?

Collect clothes and accessories that can be used for dramatic play and for dramatizations. Keep them in a special place, box, old suitcase, or trunk so that they are always readily accessible.

Encourage your children to respond to a story or character with dramatization.

Watch your children after they have watched a movie. They often act out action scenes. Use their natural interest in that particular scene to encourage additional dramatization.

After you've read a story aloud, encourage your children to act out a scene or pretend to be a character.

Turn a story into readers' theater. Select a passage that has lots of dialogue in it. Let each person take one or more roles. Pick a prop to represent each role. Practice reading the dialogue (conversation) with lots of expression. For example, if you select Peter Rabbit, one family member could wear a straw hat and carry a hoe, and read the part of the farmer. Another family member could wear an apron and glasses, and read the part of Peter's mother. Another family member could wear a blue coat and read the part of Peter. One of the appealing aspects of readers' theater is that the props can be very simple and the actors do not have to move about a stage or create background scenery. The actors can just sit around the kitchen table or on the living room floor and perform.

When you're reading a story aloud to your children, have them read or repeat the dialogue, using lots of expression.

With your children, make cards that have one character, situation, setting, or prop written on each card. Decorate an empty cereal box and place all the character cards in it. Decorate another empty cereal box and place all the situations in it. Do the same for settings and props. Have a child pick out one character, one situation, one setting, and one prop, then act them out. For example, your child might draw Little Red Riding Hood (character), downtown Cleveland (setting), hungry (situation), and box (prop). You can expand on this game by having actual items to represent each card. For example, for each character you might have a hat or article of clothing, and for each prop you might have an actual item.

Make some finger puppets out of paper or material scraps. The puppets can act out a particular story the children are familiar with, or the puppets can be used to act out a new dialogue or new story.

Find a book on puppets and discover all the different kinds of puppets and backgrounds that can be created from materials that can be found around the house.

Audiotape or videotape your children's dramatic productions or dramatic readings. If you do this often, you'll have lots of variety.

Interview your children when they are dressed up as other characters. Encourage them to answer the questions as if they were those characters.

When your children have written a story, try to act it out or dramatize it.

Dramatize stories that are part of your family history. Record them on audiotape or videotape.

This list of suggested activites is short, and is designed only as a springboard for your own ideas. Begin with an activity you can do easily and comfortably with your children. Then add those activities that work especially well for you and your children.

Grammar and Usage

In discussions about grammar and usage, grammar usually means correctness of usage. Correctness of usage involves saying, "Jim and I went shopping," instead of "Me and Jim went shopping." The debates about grammar and usage in school usually center around how and when usage is taught. Instruction in usage can range from one classroom with worksheets and grammar books in which children complete exercise after exercise focused on a single aspect of usage, to another classroom in which children are provided with many opportunities during which to practice language use and during which the teacher points out patterns of usage, using the children's language as the instructional moment. Let me elaborate on both examples.

In the first classroom, all the children are asked to complete worksheets or exercises from grammar textbooks in which a particular correct usage is highlighted. The children might be spending two weeks learning about using "I" instead of "me" as the subject of a verb, or they might spend three weeks learning the correct way to use apostrophes to indicate possession (Sam's cat). The primary mode of instruction would be the worksheet or textbook exercises, and every child, regardless of his or her knowledge of correct usage, completes the exercises.

In the second classroom, the children are engaged in a wide variety of language events throughout the day, providing the teacher with many opportunities to see and hear their language use. A young writer may need to know about quotation marks or apostrophes to show possession so that a letter is ready for sending. Two children preparing a demonstration speech may be ready to learn to use "I" instead of "me" as the subject of a verb.

In the first classroom, the moment for learning correctness in usage is predetermined by the table of contents in a textbook and the scope and sequence in a publisher's curriculum. There is no conscious correlation of the correct usage with particular children's needs or with particular situations that come up in the classroom.

In the second classroom, the moment for learning correctness in usage is determined by the children's needs, and there are immediate opportunities to apply and reinforce the newly-learned usage in situations that come up in the classroom.

An important difference between the two classroom examples is that the objective of correctness in usage in the first classroom may be limited in the children's minds to scoring well on the exercises. In the second classroom, the objective of correct usage has to do with the users' need for communicating effectively, and that objective may result in children's greater personal motivation for correctness in usage.

What can grammar and usage look like?

"This is really hard to read," Raul begins. "I mean, the story's great and all, but I can't tell when you're telling and when they're talking." "You mean those things? I should use those things like this [he draws quotation marks]?" Molly asks. "Yeah, that'd help," says Raul. "So when do you use them? Where?" Molly hands Raul her story draft. Tonio, another member of the editing group, grabs the paper. "I know. Here's how I know. See, my brother has all these comics and he said every time somebody says something you draw these things around it. It's kinda like they're a comic bubble. You know the bubble where the words are? Only you can't draw a bubble when you write so you use these instead." Molly looks unsure, so Tonio takes her story draft and starts reading it under his breath until he gets to a quote. "'Come here.' See, that's what the princess says and it comes out of her mouth like a comic bubble so you put those things there." Together, Raul, Tonio and Molly rework the draft, adding quotation marks where they're needed.

What can we do at home?

✎ Provide lots of opportunities for children to write and speak.

✎ Keep in mind that there are age-appropriate errors in correctness. Correcting an 18-month old who says, "Me go" would not be appropriate. There are also situations in which correcting usage would be counterproductive. For example, if your child is very excited about something that happened in the front yard and is telling you about it in rich detail, it would be inappropriate to interrupt the story to point out incorrect usage.

If you are unsure yourself about correctness in usage, there are three fail-safe things you can do. First, check with your children's teacher to see if there are some particular common patterns or usages you can reinforce at home. Second, provide lots of opportunities for your children to speak and to listen. Third, provide lots of opportunities for your children to read and be read to. Books are one of the richest, easiest, most accessible sources of correctness in usage.

Listen for patterns of errors. For example, your children may be consistently using "me" instead of "I" incorrectly: "Me and Jake cleaned up my room." If you correct usage, focus on a pattern error rather than correct several different errors.

Wait until your children have finished the story or message that they're telling you or writing to you before correcting the usage. Respond to their story or message first before commenting on usage.

Monitor yourself on how often you correct your children in usage. There will be many opportunities at home and at school for them to learn correct usage, but if they talk and write less because they expect correction, eventually there may be little of their writing and talking to correct.

Especially with older children, discuss the appropriateness of correctness of usage. If they want to be effective with their writing or speaking to particular audiences or in particular situations, then correctness of usage will be an important factor. With other audiences or situations, it may not be so important.

 Model correctness of usage.

 Read lots of books and poems aloud to your children.

This list of suggested activities is short, and is designed only as a springboard for your own ideas. Begin with an activity you can do easily and comfortably with your children. Then add those activities that work especially well for you and your children.

Language Acquisition

There have been volumes written about language acquisition: what it is, how it comes to be, and how it can be helped or hindered. The study of language acquisition is the study of how children acquire spoken and written language.

From birth, children are exposed to a world in which language is dominant. They hear our voices, our tones, our rhythms, our language patterns and pronunciations. They respond with sounds that imitate, and they also create new words and combinations. They see printed letters, words and phrases, and again, they respond with ones that imitate, and they also create new ones.

When children have many opportunities for hearing language, then they have many opportunities for hearing a wide range of voices, tones, rhythms, patterns, pronunciations, vocabulary, and sentence structure. When children have many opportunities for speaking, then they have many opportunities for experimenting with expressing themselves orally in a variety of effective ways. When children have many opportunities for seeing the written language, they have many opportunities for seeing a wide range of written forms, patterns, vocabulary, and sentence structures. When children have many opportunities for writing, they have many opportunities for experimenting with expressing themselves effectively in a variety of written forms, for a variety of audiences and purposes. In summary, then, the more children see and hear language, the better they are able to speak and write.

What can language acquisition look like?

The first graders had been keeping meal worms in oatmeal for two weeks. Each day, they had been drawing and writing in their science logs. Mattie piped up in frustration, "I'm tired of writing 'little white things' hundreds of times every day. Can I call 'em something else?" Mr. Meldrum chuckled. "Well," he said, "biologists must have been just as tired of writing 'little white things' as you are, because they decided to call them pupae. You can call them pupae too." "Yahoo," cheered Mattie, and turned back to writing in her science log.

What can we do at home?

Provide lots of different and frequent opportunities for your children to speak, listen, read, and write. Focus on the frequency and the variety, not on the correctness, of your children's speaking or writing.

Model frequency and variety in your own speaking, reading, and writing.

Build children's awareness of language by sharing jokes and puns.

Read lots of poetry aloud.

Think of ways to broaden your children's experiences with oral and written language. Listen with them to different radio stations. Read different magazines or newspapers with them. Point out different commercials. Choose books by a wide range of authors and about a wide range of topics and characters.

Talk, talk, talk to your children.

Listen, listen, listen to your children.

Read, read, read to your children and have them read, read, read to you.

Write, write, write to your children and have them write, write, write to you.

This list of suggested activites is short, and is designed only as a springboard for your own ideas. Begin with an activity you can do easily and comfortably with your children. Then add those activities that work especially well for you and your children.

Bilingual Education

Bilingual education literally means that the school uses two languages in its instruction. The extent to which both languages are used varies greatly from school to school and from district to district. When I was an elementary school student in Lima, Peru, my morning classes were conducted in English, my afternoon classes conducted in Spanish. In both languages we learned reading, composition, oral presentation, and the histories of Peru and the United States. Our textbooks and trade books were published in both languages. Both languages were developed equally in the language arts (reading, speaking, writing, and listening) and valued equally in both social and political contexts, regardless of which language might be a child's home language (primary language used in the home).

There are schools and classrooms in the United States where this scenario of bilingual education is played out, but the majority of classrooms limit the second language use to signs, oral directions, occasional conversation, or direct instruction confined to a set time of the day. Children whose home language is other than English are often enrolled in ESL (English as a second language) programs. These programs are discussed more fully in this book under ESL.

As other countries and peoples become easier to visit and know, and as our own country's population becomes richer with an ever-increasing diversity of peoples and languages, the allure of bilingual education becomes stronger. Bilingual education in the elementary grades is particularly appealing because school-age children can pick up second and third languages so much more quickly than adults, and the scheduling in elementary grades is more flexible than it is in the upper grades or secondary schools, thus allowing for more bilingual options.

What can bilingual education look like?

Amy looks up at the calendar and reads, *"Hoy es miércoles, el diez de febrero."* She turns to Becky. "Uh oh, Beck. Only two more days until our report's due. I only have a few notes. Can you come over tonight and work on it?" *"No sé,"* answers Becky. *"Tengo ir a la iglesia con mi hermana."* "Maestra," Amy asks the teacher in a sudden panic, *"dónde están los libros de nuestro grupo?"* "Over there on the round table," answers Ms. Milham.

What can we do at home?

Have your librarian help you locate books that are written in other languages. There are many children's favorites that have been printed in more than one language. If your children know the English version, they will be able to understand the version written in a different language.

Begin with language books that teach numbers or familiar words such as home and school words.

Model a receptive attitude toward other languages.

Listen to radio stations that broadcast in other languages.

Attend special events sponsored by groups from other countries that feature ethnic food and customs.

Find out about second language opportunities offered through your community center.

Ask your friends if they know other languages. They can help you and your children learn some simple words and phrases. Ask them to speak another language around your children so that your children can hear the sounds of another language.

Begin by learning numbers or simple words of another language. Short phrases in which you can substitute single words are helpful (Here is a pen. Here is a book. Here is a chair.).

Select songs or short conversations in another language that you and your children can learn. Audio recordings may be available at your local library.

✎   Go back into your own family background and find out if there are other languages represented. You may want to begin by learning one of those languages. You may already have in your family special vocabulary words whose origins are in another language.

✎   If you or your children already speak another language, keep it up. You may have to make a conscious effort to do so, and may even have to schedule a time period each day or special days each week when everyone in the family will speak that language.

This list of suggested activites is short, and is designed only as a springboard for your own ideas. Begin with an activity you can do easily and comfortably with your children. Then add those activities that work especially well for you and your children.

ESL (English as a Second Language)

Although the United States is a country in which hundreds of languages thrive, many since before the introduction of English, the fact is that the dominant language in most communities is English. Schools are faced with the task of teaching English as a second language to those children whose home language is other than English. The school's instructional approach may be English only, with no attention or support given to the home language; English, with support given to parallel development of the home language; or some mix of the preceding two approaches. Additionally, the children may be scheduled full time in the regular classroom, or they may be pulled out of the regular classroom for scheduled instruction in English. The variations of ESL instruction, then, are myriad, and there are rationales and theories for each variation.

The factors that are taken into consideration when designing an ESL program for students include school and district resources (money, scheduling, staff, etc.); the degree of value placed on the home language; and the adoption of a particular theory of language acquisition or second-language acquisition.

In some classrooms, children are immersed in an English-only environment—left to sink or swim in the new language—and receive whatever special instruction is possible, given the teacher's class load (number of students and time for class preparation). In addition to this classroom situation, the children may be pulled out for part of the day to receive special instruction in English as a second language. Unfortunately, though, while the children are receiving special instruction in English, they are also missing interaction with classmates and instruction that is continuing in the regular classroom.

In other classrooms, the class load, resources, and perhaps even the teacher's second language allow for limited-English-speaking children to remain in the regular classroom and be supported in their acquisition of English.

In either case, whether the children remain in the regular classroom full time or are pulled out for special instruction, the question of whether the home language is valued is very important. Devaluing children's home language makes strong statements about how we regard those children as individuals, their parents and ancestry, and the children's personal and ethnic histories.

Building English as a second language can be accomplished positively and with astonishing results when the home language is not

Nathan Johlas, age 2

only used as a bridge to English, but is supported in its development as a separate language.

What can ESL look like?

Second grader Luki has a stack of note cards on the kitchen table. She looks toward the sink where her sister is peeling carrots, turns back to the note cards, and prints in large letters the word "sink." She looks around the kitchen again, turns back to the note cards, and fills out three more note cards in large print: "cupboard, refrigerator, counter." "That's enough for tonight," she says aloud. "Mama!" she calls, "I have tonight's lesson ready!" Mama comes in. *"Is 't klaar?"* she asks Luki. "Yes, Mama, but first, let's review the ones I taught you yesterday. Then I'll test you and if you get them all right, I'll give you a hug. What is this?" and she points to the chair. "That is a chair," answers Mama, well on her way to a hug.

What can we do at home?

Ask your children's teachers about the ESL programs at school.

Ask if there are ways you and/or your children can be supportive of children enrolled in the ESL classes.

REANDING

"I want my child to be a good reader." What do we mean by that? Perhaps decades ago, we might have meant that we wanted our children to say the word "dog" when they saw the three letters "d," "o," and "g" on a page. And today, we certainly want our children to be able to do that when they are reading. But the demands of today's world of reading are much more complex than that.

From birth, our children are immersed in a world that is rich in talk and print. **Emergent literacy** is the way young children make sense of all the sounds and symbols that they see and hear and touch. **Environmental print** is in the home and beyond the home, but it is not simply information. Environmental print can be used to influence and persuade even very young children. And when print and nonprint media combine in all their alluring, captivating forms, children can be entertained, informed, and seduced long before they ever enter a classroom. **Media literacy**, then, becomes crucial, not simply as a means of introducing children to the wide range of print and nonprint media that provide entertainment and information, but as a means of helping children become critical of the uses of media, for their own purposes as well as the purposes of others.

Story has always been an integral part of human life and tradition, and is still so today. The proliferation of **children's literature**, both fiction and nonfiction, has opened countless worlds of information and experience to children. Children will have to use their own critical skills to select from the endless choices according to their own interests and purposes.

Emergent Literacy

Emergent literacy is different from what we generally think of as reading readiness. Reading readiness traditionally involves listing a set of specific skills (for example, knowing left to right, knowing letter–sound correspondence) that children need to master before they are ready to learn to read, and then designing instruction so that children master those specific skills. Although proponents of programs with a reading readiness focus and proponents of programs with an emergent literacy focus might appear to agree on a goal of having children who can read, the goals of instruction based on a child's emergent literacy are much broader than simply preparing the children to read. Emergent literacy is a much broader way of thinking about children's interaction with many different aspects of language and literacy.

Homes and classrooms that are most supportive of emergent literacy are those that provide many different kinds of opportunities for children to speak, hear, read, write, view, and think.

Emergent literacy takes into account our speaking and listening to children, and our providing rich oral language experiences for them.

Emergent literacy takes into account the children's active participation as writers and readers in a print world that is such an integral part of their daily lives, and acknowledges the children's earliest reading and writing interactions with that print world. Emergent literacy takes into account the children's dispositions to being active, purposeful language users; and that the children will proceed through emergent literacy at different rates, in different ways, and through different experiences.

As you will see in the following vignette, emergent literacy for me was a pathway into fanciful worlds of heroines and shape shifters. Emergent literacy was my pathmaker through the literate world I called "home" and the print- and talk-rich world beyond my home.

Billy Grider, age 7

What can emergent literacy look like?

One of my earliest memories is that of sitting on my parents' laps and being read to. Sometimes I chose the book, often I helped hold it and turn the pages—carefully so that the corners wouldn't wrinkle and bend. Sometimes the cue to turn the page was a pause. Sometimes I remembered where the turning spot was from numerous other readings of the same book. Sometimes there was no cue but I just couldn't wait to see the illustration on the next page. Fairy tales were my favorites. As the words on the page were read aloud, they conjured up visions of patient, virtuous, and beautiful heroines. These heroines shared the crags and haunted woods with leagues of shape shifters and other sympathetic creatures eager to help the heroines overcome obstacles that only the meanest of ogres and cruelest of stepmothers could throw in their path. But the lap I sat upon and the arms encircling me to hold the book kept me safe from any real danger. And while those visions were transporting me to other worlds, the words that conjured up those visions became my words. I probably recognized the words "happily ever after" in print long before I recognized my own last name, "Hydrick."

What can we do at home?

✏️ Read aloud to your children. Hold them on your lap...or have them hold you on their laps!

✏️ Have your children read aloud to you. They can retell familiar books or memorized favorites or create stories for picture books or their own pictures.

✏️ Read all sorts of material aloud: billboards, signs, flyers, brochures, letters, commercials, ads, magazines, newspapers, comics.

✏️ Read material to your children that is not necessarily kids' stuff. If the children never hear big words like "gargantuan" and "nutrition," they'll have trouble figuring them out later in their own reading.

Create a special snuggle place or have a special snuggle chair for reading.

Create fun places for reading aloud. For example, during the summer, bring last year's leaky plastic wading pool inside, fill it with lots of pillows and stuffed animals, and snuggle up to read aloud.

Find out what your children's favorite books are and read them, but keep introducing new characters, new authors, new genres (mystery, animal, science fiction, etc.).

When you're reading aloud, use that context to help children learn letters and letter-sound relationships.

Encourage your children to respond to literature by dancing, dramatizing, drawing, or discussing. Together, make finger puppets or a shadow box or a diorama. Act out a story in the sandbox or in the tub.

Encourage your child to write daily. There are lots of wonderful pads of paper and bound blank books to choose from. Children can add their own illustrations, photographs, or pictures cut from magazines and newspapers. You can have your children dictate to you and you can ask for their help with writing an occasional letter (begin with the initial letters in their names).

Set up a message center where each day you write a short message to your children. It can be a question that your children will find the answer to during the day. It can be telling them what's for breakfast, or who's coming to visit, or where you're going in the car that day.

Secretly place coupons under their pillows or in their pockets for hugs, kisses, a glass of chocolate milk, or a story.

Have your children design a bookmark or a bookplate. Let them design door hangers to announce that there is a readaloud in progress or an author at work.

Write a story together in which you and your children take turns writing words and pictures to make a rebus story, where pictures are substituted for a word or sound. You could use a picture from a magazine, a family photograph, or a child's drawing as the starter for your story.

Cut up large words and letters from magazines and newspapers and help your children paste them together to create words, phrases, or messages.

For dessert, have your children write messages in pudding.

Create texture words: glue rice on paper to form words, sew letters on material, cut out sandpaper, glue foam peanuts on paper to form letters or words.

Share the writing of your grocery or shopping list with your children. They can embellish with illustrations. When you arrive at the store, have your children help you look for the words or the products on the shelves. You might go to the soup section of the store and have your children find all the words that say "soup."

Label lots of things in the house. Make cards with the label words on them and have your children match cards with labels.

Link your children's lives with the contents of books. Before or after a special family event (trip, wedding, birthday), go to the local library and find books that have pictures and information about similar events.

Draw a map of your neighborhood or buy a city map so that your children can see your street name and names of other familiar streets.

Decorate a t-shirt to celebrate a book. Use markers or fabric paints on a real shirt, or cut out the shape of a t-shirt from paper. Hang lots of paper t-shirts that have book celebrations on them from a string across your children's bedrooms or down the hallway.

Instead of using the t-shirt shape, make squares with pictures of scenes or characters from favorite books and make a large book quilt out of paper or material.

Have your children help you make a television list of programs the family will watch for the day or for the week.

Cover a box with brightly colored wrapping paper and fill it with leftover, unmatched writing paper and envelopes. Toss in a few unusual pens or pencils that have odd shapes or tops or colors, and add some stickers or small pictures that can be glued on the paper. Keep the box as a special writing center.

This list of suggested activities is short, and is designed only as a springboard for your own ideas. Begin with an activity you can do easily and comfortably with your children. Then add those activities that work especially well for you and your children.

Environmental Print

Environmental print is the variety of texts that are part of our world or environment: exit signs, street signs, billboards, labels on cans and boxes of food, words on game boards, and so on. Very early, children are able to identify environmental print and add it to their personal word banks by using such clues as colors, pictures, letter shapes, and word conformation. Environmental print is responsible for early learning of words such as "exit," "start," "on," "off," "stop," and "McDonald's" or "Pizza Hut."

Parents and primary teachers can build on children's personal word banks of environmental print by labeling all sorts of objects in the home and classroom. Children in a kindergarten class soon learn that the word on the water-splattered sign near where they wash their hands is "sink." A preschooler soon learns that the same word on the front door, bathroom door, and bedroom door is "door."

Children who enter kindergarten may or may not know their alphabet, but they have already acquired a foundation of words upon which reading phrases and sentences can be built, and from which the children can begin to recognize patterns in sounds.

What can environmental print look like?

Michael bounces up and down in the grocery cart seat, points excitedly at the entrance to the store and sings, "Everyone out of the exit door, the exit door, the exit door." Aunt Marg joins in the song and they finish together, clapping for themselves. "Hurrah for Michael," says Aunt Marg, "I'm so proud of you." They continue down the aisle. Occasionally, Michael points to a can or box and says, "Mmmm, Aunt Marg," not because he thinks the contents are delicious, but because the label has a word that begins with the first letter of his name, although Aunt Marg has told him that Michael, Marg, and delicious things are all "Mmm, mmm, good."

What can we do at home?

✎ Label lots of things around the home. Involve your children in the labeling.

✎ Help your children start scrapbooks of favorite words. One scrapbook can be pages filled with labels from favorite food packages. One scrapbook can be pages filled with headlines about a favorite sports team or player.

✎   Play identification games to call attention to the great variety of environment print. Who will be the first one to see the word "exit"? to see "stop"? "sale"?

✎   Take a newspaper article and a bright marker. Have your children circle all the words or letters they know. Or you can write or cut out one word ("sale," for example), place it in front of them, and have them circle the word each time they find that word in the article.

This list of suggested activites is short, and is designed only as a springboard for your own ideas. Begin with an activity you can do easily and comfortably with your children. Then add those activities that work especially well for you and your children.

Trade Books

Trade books are the books you and your children buy or check out of the library and read. When I began teaching first grade in 1966, my small classroom library included *Where the Wild Things Are*, *Frog and Toad*, several books by Dr. Seuss, and, of course, Caldecott winners (outstanding picture books) for each year. There has been such a proliferation of children's trade books in the past decade, though, that a first-grade classroom today could have thousands of wonderful books and add hundreds each year. The array of nonfiction and fiction books is mindboggling and absolutely glorious. Regardless of their age, children love to listen to stories, and today's ever-increasing treasure of publications offers something for anyone's taste and for any situation.

When children are read to by family members and teachers, they hear the wonders of our language, increase their vocabulary and their patterns and variations of language, and also increase their store of knowledge. When a teacher reads aloud to the class, the children can be motivated to read another book by the same author or a book about a similar subject. Reading aloud to all ages of children enhances their oral language and, eventually, their own reading abilities. Reading and being read to broaden children's writing by adding to their choices in vocabulary, characters, events, settings, sentence variation, and perspectives.

Trade books are the primary contents of libraries and bookstores. Trade books could be the primary contents of the classroom. Trade books are the friends you take home, hold, read, and listen to again and again. They take you to other countries, other galaxies, other times. They make you cry, laugh, giggle, grin, and sigh. They're with you on a park bench, in a quiet corner, or on the subway. They're one of the best reasons to sit on a lap, to cuddle, and to share.

What can trade books look like?

It was the fourth graders' second overnight in the library. The boys were camped in nonfiction, the girls in picture books. Junko, Akiko, and Dawn were crowded into a zipped-up sleeping bag with one flashlight and two of Alvin Schwartz's collections of scary stories. They were practicing for the ghost story session that would take place outside under the ramada at midnight. Two weeks ago, Maggie and Violet had talked Rudine into reading Mildred Taylor's *The Gold Cadillac* with them. Reading the short story had evolved into a long project when the girls decided to interview grandparents, aunts, and uncles who had had similar frightening experiences in the south during the 1950s and '60s. Tonight, with no limits on how many books they could check out, they laid out all of Taylor's books in a row and sorted them chronologically. Violet had worked out a reading schedule for them, and they would begin *Mississippi River* at 3 AM. Asante's mother was in a rocking chair in the reference corner, reading aloud some of her favorite poems. Even with an audience of seven fourth graders, each poem had initiated a comment such as, "Oh, I love that one!" or "I know that one!" or "My mom reads that one to me!"

What can we do at home?

Libraries are your largest-volume, cheapest source of trade books. You can go home with armloads, trade them for different armloads the next day or week or month, and at most libraries, it doesn't cost a penny.

✎   Check with your local bookstores to find out when authors will come for signings. Signed books are always special, and children can have the opportunity of exchanging a few words with the author.

✎   Libraries and bookstores often have lists available to give you an idea of books that are appropriate for different age levels or are award winners. Books that have received awards have been chosen for specific reasons, such as illustrations or story quality.

✎   Use trade books, both fiction and nonfiction, to support your children's interests in hobbies or specific topics.

This list of suggested activites is short, and is designed only as a springboard for your own ideas. Begin with an activity you can do easily and comfortably with your children. Then add those activities that work especially well for you and your children.

Pattern Books
Predictable Books

Pattern books and predictable books are ones in which the readers use their understanding of patterns in text or illustration to predict the next section of text or illustration. But enduring, favorite pattern books and predictable books go beyond the notion of filling in a single sound so that words rhyme or match other words in sound (The ant can't pant.). These books encourge the readers to use their understanding of patterns in aspects such as context, picture clues, story line, language rhythm, and syntax to predict what the author or illustrator will provide next.

Twenty years after Michael first read *Green Eggs and Ham* and other Seuss favorites to himself, our family will still question one another with something like, "Could you, would you, in a box? with a fox? with no socks?" We might express gratitude by saying, "Thank you, thank you, Sam-I-am," or conclude a conversation with "Dum ditty dum ditty dum dum dum." Those word patterns from children's books have become part of our family's vocabulary tradition.

What can pattern books and predictable books look like?

With each of those aspects in which books could be termed pattern or predictable, there is the assumption on the part of the author or illustrator that the young reader will have had the kinds of visual and language experiences that would lead him or her to an appropriate prediction. For example, Suki might write a book for her little brother. On the first page, there is the text, "Something's there behind the rock. Do you know what it is?" The illustration is of a rock with a horse's tail showing. Turn the page and the illustration shows the horse hiding behind the rock with its tail showing. The text reads, "You're right, of course, it is a horse." On the next page, there is the text, "Something's there behind the rock. Do you know what it is?" The illustration is of the same rock with a cat's tail showing. Turn the page and the illustration shows the cat hiding behind the rock with its tail showing. The text reads, "You're right. It's that. It is a cat." You and Suki's little brother already know that the next page will begin with the text, "Something's there behind the rock. Do you know what it is?" You'll both be looking for the visual clue poking out behind the rock. Once you've figured out the animal, you'll both be expecting the text, "You're right." Then, depending on your experience with rhyming, you may or may not be able to guess what the rhyming phrase for the hiding animal is. Regardless of whether or not you were able to guess the correct rhyming word, you'll be rewarded with the rhyming answer. Suki's book has incorporated several of the ways pattern or predictable books can build on what young readers already know about language and pictures. The end of Suki's book shows a strangely colored, odd-shaped tail behind the rock. "Something's there behind the rock. Do you know what it is?" When you turn the page, there is a fanciful monster and this text: "You're right. You betcha. Now he's gonna come and getcha!" She finished the book with a delightful mix of the predictable and the unexpected.

What can we do at home?

✎ Find a wide variety of pattern or predictable books. Alternate books that use picture clues with books that use patterns in syllable number, context, story line, language rhythm, syntax.

✎ Children love to have good pattern and predictable books read over and over again. Let your children tell you what the patterns are. Give enough wait time for your children to guess what might come next.

✎ You can write pattern and predictable books for your children or with your children. Use words and phrases that they love, and use photographs or pictures from magazines and newspapers. For example, make a collection of four or five family photos. Glue each one on a page of paper and tape a piece of paper over each photo so that the paper can be lifted to reveal the photo. Leave just a little corner of the photo showing so that the children will be able to guess which photo it is. Then write a pattern of text over each one, such as, "Stephanie's family loves to play. What are they doing together on this day?" Soon, your children will be reading the text over each photo all by themselves.

This list of suggested activities is short, and is designed only as a springboard for your own ideas. Begin with an activity you can do easily and comfortably with your children. Then add those activities that work especially well for you and your children.

Literature-Based Reading Programs

L iterature-based reading programs can look very different from each other. The characteristic common to all of them, however, is that literature is used in some way as instructional material. The literature can be presented as trade books or as anthologies within which there could be excerpts and complete works. Support for the literature can cover a wide range of materials and activities, including audiotapes and videotapes, computer software and CD-ROM, puppets and costumes, companion books, home-connection materials, classroom and home support activities, worksheets and workbooks. The support materials and activities can be teacher-made, student-made, or commercially pre-pared.

Literature-based programs can be assessed in many different ways, too. Some assessment methods focus more on the separate reading skills (decoding, for example), while other assessment methods focus more on the content of the literature itself such as character develop-ment and author's craft. Some assessments may be conducted with machine-scored answer sheets. Other assessments may be done through anecdotal records of literature group discussions, journal responses, and dramatizations.

Literature-based reading programs can reflect a combination of any or all of the presentations of literature, materials and activities, and assessment methods presented above. The decisions that define how the literature-based program will look are made at state and local levels and involve school boards, administrators, teachers, and often parents and students.

For the convenience of describing them, I've divided literature-based reading programs into four general categories. However, these divisions do not exist clearly in the world of classrooms. Each school and each teacher will select characteristics and methods which best suit the unique student populations in each classroom.

Literature-based reading programs can be ones in which the literature included in the reading program is written and/or selected for the specific purpose of instructing the children in a particular skill. The literature in these programs is simply the medium through which the children learn skills. Typically, the drill materials are skill-specific and extensive.

Literature-based reading programs can be ones in which the children read from anthologies of literature that are provided by textbook companies. The anthologies can be collections of trade books that have been selected by the textbook company, or the anthologies can be combinations of complete works and excerpts. Typically, there are drill materials such as workbooks that accompany the anthologies. The anthologies are packaged according to a specified grade level or reading level that the children in the class or reading group are expected to have in common when they are placed with that anthology.

Literature-based reading programs can be ones in which children read trade books in small groups, large groups, as a total class, or as individuals. At any given time, the children can be engaged in one or more of these group configurations and with one or more trade books, depending on student interest and purpose as well as teacher interest and purpose.

Literature-based reading programs can be ones in which literature is introduced into the classroom curriculum as it relates to themes or topics that the class is studying. For example, if the class is studying the westward movement in the United States, then the children might be reading the speeches of Chief Joseph of the Nez Perce, a collection of homesteaders' letters, or tall tales about Paul Bunyan and Pecos Bill.

What can a literature-based reading program look like?

"We'll be right back," says Akiko. "Celia and I can't find Derek and he's reading *Matilda* with us." They trot off to find the fifth member of their literature study group. Today is a crucial one for their group because they're going to decide how they'd like to dramatize the first miracle in the book. They agreed that it was a turning point in the book for the character Matilda and wanted to think of a way to illustrate the differences in Matilda's situation before and after the miracle. This particular group has been together for four months and has already completed six of Roald Dahl's novels. They've contracted with the librarian to complete several projects about Dahl that can be placed in the library for checkout by other classrooms. They've read literature by many authors in the same time period, often in other literature study groups, but their fondness for Dahl's books keeps bringing them back together as a group.

What can we do at home?

✎   Ask your children's teachers how literature is used in the classroom. Ask how you can support the classroom literature program with home activities.

✎   Volunteer to go in your children's classroom or library and read literature aloud to individual students or small groups.

✎   Regardless of how literature is or is not used in your children's classroom, you can make literature the base of your reading program at home. Provide lots of opportunities for your children to read and listen to literature. Make frequent trips to the library, explore secondhand book stores, create a special library space at home.

✎   Encourage your children to make posters of favorite books, authors, characters, and scenes. Decorate bedrooms, bathrooms, hallways, and reading areas with the posters.

✎   Cover boxes with bright paper and fill with literature about a special animal or place or topic. For example, cover a box with Snoopy wrapping paper and fill it with literature (fiction and nonfiction) about dogs. Fill a gift bag that has crayons on it with literature about artists.

This list of suggested activites is short, and is designed only as a springboard for your own ideas. Begin with an activity you can do easily and comfortably with your children. Then add those activities that work especially well for you and your children.

Response to Literature

When we look at a reader's response to literature, we are looking at the interaction between the reader and a piece of literature. It's easy to see why we feel that each reader who reads *Peter Rabbit*, for example, is a little different from every other reader. Each reader has had a unique set of experiences, and those experiences will influence how the reader responds to the story. First-grader Nadia and her parents, for example, live in the country and have a problem with wild rabbits coming through the fence and nibbling the food supply that will get Nadia's family through the winter. Celia lives in downtown Phoenix and for her, rabbits are delightful furry little creatures she can pet and squeeze at the state fair and at the zoo. Nadia's response and Celia's response to the story will be very different from one another. If Celia moves from downtown Phoenix to a rural setting such as Nadia's, she may read the same *Tale of Peter Rabbit* and have a different response from the one she had when she lived in downtown Phoenix. After moving to the country, Celia will probably understand in a different way about vegetables growing in rows or out of the ground instead of a grocery bin, and she may respond differently to the pictures of the hoe and the wheelbarrow after having touched them and used them herself. In these examples, the words written on the pages of *Peter Rabbit* have not changed at all, but they have meant very different things to Nadia and to Celia. Both girls can also read about Beatrix Potter, the author, and about her life and fascination with rabbits. Will that also help change their interpretation of *Peter Rabbit*? It might.

Response to literature in the classroom involves many considerations. Children respond individually to literature, and in the classroom, they are provided with opportunities to respond to literature in small and large groups, sharing their ideas and learning about other children's ideas. Through this sharing of ideas, children learn that literature can mean many things to many people and that within that range of many meanings, the meaning each child derives is included.

Classrooms often provide a wide variety of media through which children can respond to literature. For example, they may respond initially to a story by acting it out, by dancing, or by creating a project that represents a character or scene or event. In fact, the more varied the media are for response, the greater the likelihood that each child's particular strength in expression will be tapped into at some point. Also, seeing the same piece of literature reflected in a diorama, a skit, a poster, and a dance can add a great deal of depth to the children's understanding of that single piece of literature.

Teachers might have the children listen to or read a piece of literature for the sheer enjoyment of it, for information, or they might engage the children in analyzing the genre, the author's craft, characters, the effect of setting, or any of the myriad other elements of literature. The children's responses will reflect the purpose of the reading.

With literature response, it's important to keep in mind that there are as many responses to a single piece of literature as there are readers of that one piece. Additionally, there are as many forms for response as there are ways that people have for expressing themselves.

What can response to literature look like?

Before I have even finished reading "and they lived happily ever after," Libby has hopped off my lap and is dancing around the room, singing. "I'm beautiful! My hair's beautiful! My shoes are beautiful! My mouth's beautiful! My hand's beautiful!" Suddenly, she drops to the floor on her back, arms and legs spread out. "Aaugh! The wicked witch put a spell on me." She remains still for at least ten seconds. Later that day, at the dinner table, the prince (knife) battles the wicked witch (fork) to save the beautiful princess (spoon) who is lying bewitched but beautiful in a mound of mashed potatoes.

What can we do at home?

Ask your children's teachers about the ways children are encouraged to respond to literature in the classroom.

When you're reading to your children, share with them your responses to the literature. Do you respond the same way as your children do? differently? Talk about what experiences might have led you to respond the same way or in a different way. Note how you share your responses and how you respond to your children's interpretations. Are you being open to varied responses? How wide a range of response are you encouraging?

Think of as many different ways as you can for children to respond to literature. Sit down with your children and brainstorm a list. If they haven't tried dancing lately, encourage them to give it a shot. If they haven't tried puppets lately, prepare a box with some great puppet materials (sticks, felt, eyes, yarn, socks) and let them make puppets for a specific story.

Read a book that's been made into a movie. Discuss with your children the movie scriptwriter's, director's, or actors' responses to the story and compare them with your children's response or your own response.

Read materials together with your children that they may not be able to read independently. Their oral vocabulary may exceed their reading vocabulary to an astonishing degree! Then discuss what you're reading. Find out what they know. Find out what they make connections to in their own experiences.

Keep an index card file that all family members can add to. Write the title of the piece of literature at the top and have each family member write a short response or draw an illustration as response to the literature. Are the responses different? Do they change over time?

Keep a shoe box of responses to a particular author, genre, or piece of literature. How different and how alike are the responses?

Follow up with a piece of literature that your children have read in their school classroom. Encourage them to respond in a very different way.

Have your children respond to the same piece of literature with a different point of view. For example, have them respond to the story of Cinderella as the stepmother might have.

This list of suggested activities is short, and is designed only as a springboard for your own ideas. Begin with an activity you can do easily and comfortably with your children. Then add those activities that work especially well for you and your children.

Media Literacy

When I was in school, print media in the classroom was primarily books, with magazines and an occasional newspaper reserved for reading as a special treat in the library. Nonprint media in the classroom included some records, mostly used in music classes or to create mood or background; and a rare 16mm black-and-white film. Most of my nonprint media experience was at home with records, radio, and photographs. Movies were a rare treat at home too, and for them we went to the local movie theater. Today, we and our children are treated to a delightful array of print media, nonprint media, and multimedia in the classroom and at home that includes videotape, computers, radio, film, virtual reality, audiotape, CD-ROM, books that pop out or have sound effects, and magazines by the hundreds for every inclination and age.

When I was in school, materials in print were designated for instruction, and nonprint materials were regarded as treats. In today's classrooms, teachers can use a wide range of print and nonprint media and multimedia presentations to present new information, to reinforce concepts in progress, or to conduct or record assessments. Instructional and recreational materials in the classroom may be print, nonprint, or a combination of both.

In today's classrooms, first graders can create audiotapes and videotapes to illustrate their understanding. Third graders can scan and use HyperCard to create their own electronic portfolios for assessment. Kindergartners author their own books, and fourth graders can author their own software programs. Classmates in multiage classrooms can create their own multimedia presentation to culminate a total-group study of Alaska, combining student drawings and photographs, student-written text, singing, dancing, dramatizations, and artifacts with materials that are commercially prepared or collected from neighborhood resources.

In today's classrooms, media literacy can range from exposure to a variety of media (videos, film, audio, computers, for example); to a study of materials presented in particular kinds of media (such as multimedia encyclopedias); to a study of the effects of media on the material (comparing the book to the movie); to a study of the effects of media on the audience. Students have come a long way from simply being entertained by nonprint media, as I was, to studying the art and techniques of nonprint media as well as the effects of nonprint media on material and audience. To today's students, then, nonprint media is less of a wonder and more of a tool for their own learning and expression.

What can media literacy look like?

Family members were streaming into the media center. Three fifth graders shared each of the twelve tables that were strewn with papers, books, and projects representing nine weeks' worth of study in language arts, science, social studies, math, music, health, and anything else that could be squeezed into a school day. Sheridan and Ishu were pulling their parents into the adjoining computer lab. Coaxing his mother into the seat in front of monitor #7, Sheridan said, "Just push 'return,' Mom. It's all set. I did it myself. Ishu too. You're gonna love it." The screen faded to a photograph of Sheridan, grinning widely and holding a self-drawn map of North America with different regions in different colors. The haunting notes of a Navajo flute provided a musical introduction. Sheridan watched his mother's face as the recording of his voice rose over the flute. "Native Americans occupied every region of the United States in 1492." For the next ten minutes, Sheridan's mother watched and listened as Sheridan's voice told the story of Native American tribes in North America through a series of photographs, drawings, and video clips, some commercially prepared and some created by Sheridan and his classmates.

What can we do at home?

Ask your children's teachers about the variety of print media that are being used in the classrooms and how they are being used.

Ask your children's teachers about the variety of nonprint media that are being used in the classrooms and how they are being used. Ask your children what they like or don't like about these media.

✎ Visit stores where there are televisions and computers and other recreational electronic devices. What are the effects of the medium or device on your children? What are some of the newest developments in media and media combinations?

✎ Log your family's media events (engagement with print and nonprint media) for a week. How much time is spent watching television? reading? listening to the radio? Note also the amount of interaction there was with the medium or with other people. Was there any follow-up (discussion or other response) after the media event? Discuss the log with your family. You may want to add more media events of a particular kind (schedule family reading time after dinner, for example), or you may want to increase the personal interaction during and after each event (ask your children some questions after they see a movie or link part of the movie to a book they've read about a similar character or topic, for example).

✎ Analyze media presentations with your children. For example, after watching a Nike commercial, talk about the combination of action and words and music. Watch commercials with the sound off or listen to commercials without watching them and talk about the difference in effectiveness. Are radio commercials written differently from television commercials? Are both different from magazine and newspaper commercials?

✎ With older children especially, discuss the subtle messages, both text and visual, on commercials such as those for cigarettes.

✎ After you've seen a movie together, talk about how the music and lighting helped to create a happy, sad, or scary mood.

✎ Go to the local library with your children and look at all the different kinds of magazines and newspapers available. Talk about the differences in picture and text. For example, the

Wall Street Journal has very few pictures, Newsweek has more. Talk about political cartoons as a medium for portraying a strong message. Talk about comic strips as a medium for portraying messages.

This list of suggested activites is short, and is designed only as a springboard for your own ideas. Begin with an activity you can do easily and comfortably with your children. Then add those activities that work especially well for you and your children.

WRITING

Writing is basically recording thoughts and ideas so that other people can read them. In today's classrooms, writing includes everything from handwriting to word processing, everything from copying words to making lists to writing letters to writing research reports. Teaching manuscript (printing) and cursive handwriting usually focuses on legibility (can it be read or deciphered), and different schools are open to some variation in the formation of letters, particularly capital or upper-case letters. When the writing is done with a typewriter or word processor, then legibility is less of a factor, so the writer is freer to indulge in special features such as different fonts, sizes of letters, and style. For example, a young writer using a word processor might select a calligraphy-type font in a large size for the cover of a collection of poetry. The same young writer could easily select **bold** or *italic* to emphasize a word or phrase in a story or report. A young writer using pen or pencil can also alter font, style, and size, but a word processor makes it much easier to do.

Today's writers are expected to be able to accomplish a great deal more than the proper formation of letters. Today's writers are expected to use composition (the creation of written text) to

- organize needs and thoughts in lists,
- communicate through business and informal letters,
- share information in reports,
- affect others through narrative (storytelling), and
- actually understand and influence their own thinking processes by writing.

Writing programs today teach children about the many

- *forms* that writing can take (letters, brochures, poems, and tall tales, for example),
- *purposes* that writing can have (to persuade, to amuse, or to inform, for example), and
- *audiences* that writing can have (self, friend, or senator, for example).

The science journal entry that a child writes to record observations about a mouse's progress in maze training will look very different from a letter that the same child might write to a grandmother to thank her for a birthday gift, and both pieces of writing will look very different from a final report that the child has written and will share with the class on the life of Harriet Tubman, Underground Railroad conductor during the Civil War. The child will need to know the appropriateness of handwriting, usage, and spelling for each piece of writing. That is, the child will need to know that although the journal entry doesn't need to be correct in terms of handwriting, usage, and spelling, the report does. How correct the letter to the grandmother is in terms of handwriting, usage, and spelling will depend on the child's relationship to the grandmother and knowing what the grandmother's expectations are.

There are many techniques that teachers use to encourage young writers to explore the greatest variety of forms, purposes, and audiences for their writing. The more children write, the more they feel that they can write. The more forms, purposes, and audiences the children experiment with, the more choices they have when they are confronted in their lives with a need to write inside and outside of the classroom. The more conscious children become of changes that need to be made in their writing and why those changes need to be made, the more control children take of their own writing.

This section will focus on classroom practices that deal with composition rather than the legibility of handwriting. We'll look into five techniques of writing instruction that engage children in a wide range of tasks and products: **writing workshop, process writing, invented spelling, freewriting,** and **poetry.**

Writing Workshop

The term **writing workshop** includes a wide range of classroom practices. The common thread in all these practices, though, is that children and teachers look at writing as an ongoing, recursive process (going back, relooking), rather than a linear one whereby the writer completes a document in a single sitting. In classrooms where there is writing workshop, children have a particular time that is designated for writing during the school day. During the writing workshop time, the teacher will probably (1) begin with a short "mini" lesson; (2) provide time for the children to write while the teacher circulates, giving one-on-one help and conferences; then (3) provide opportunity at the end of the workshop for children to share and give each other peer review and help. Let me elaborate on those three components.

In a mini-lesson, the teacher focuses on a particular point of writing. For example, if several of the children have been engaged in writing poetry, the teacher might spend a few minutes focusing on similes and metaphors. Or if a focus on letter writing is appropriate, the teacher might spend a few minutes on characteristics such as variations in format and tone (friendly or more formal). A mini-lesson on story mapping (outlining characters, setting, and events) might help children analyze and develop their own narratives or stories.

During the children's writing time, the teacher is available for immediate needs: for example, serving as a "living dictionary" for spelling, as a "living thesaurus" for varying vocabulary (using "murmured" or "shrieked" instead of "said"), or as a source for suggestions on formatting and mechanics. The children or teacher might also use this time to schedule a short writing conference in which a particular writing project or a particular writing need is discussed. A child might need help with the resolution (ending) in an almost-completed story, or a child might need a conference that focuses on incorporating descriptive language (describing a soft, warm puppy with a pink, speckled nose). During this period of the writing workshop, the children may be working on a piece for the first time or on a piece they have been revising (changing) and developing for several writing workshops. Within the environment of a writing workshop, children are encouraged to rework pieces and apply their evolving skills of revisiting and revising to develop a document which is very different from what might come out of a one-time 20- or 30-minute response to a writing prompt such as, "What did you do last summer?"

Today's classroom authors are more aware of purpose and audience than we were in school. They also have well-earned pride in what they have written. After all, within the environment of the writing workshop, they have invested time and effort into improving their writing and coming up with an effective piece of writing, whether it's a poem, a letter, a report, or any other form of writing. It is natural, then, that the children would want the opportunity to share. The classroom authors may share either a finished product or a work in progress. With either piece, their fellow authors can respond aesthetically or critically: that is, they can respond by telling how they liked the piece, or they can offer suggestions on the strengths and weaknesses of the piece.

Shalinka Huffman, age 8

Whatever the particular project or purpose might be for a day's writing workshop, the workshop environment encourages the classroom authors to treat the writing they do as serious, continuing work.

What can writing workshop look like?

It's 9 o'clock. All the children know that for the next hour, they'll be in writing workshop. Writing folders are passed out. Shane has a list of topics he's been brainstorming. He's decided on a disaster, but isn't sure whether he wants to write about his broken arm or the death of his dog. He talks it over with Choong Sang, who convinces him that he has a lot more to say about his broken arm. Julissa, Bernice, and Lupe take turns reading their story drafts to each other, giggling when something doesn't make sense, or when Lupe's prince kisses the princess. Karl is coloring the cover to his report on the Apaches. Asante has a great idea for setting out the cafeteria tables in a different way. He recruits Josh and David to help him. Should they write a letter to the janitor or schedule a conference with the principal? If they make a diagram, what should they put on it? While I work with Krissa and Solomon on using quotation marks, I can see Brandon signing up for a conference with me. I'm sure he wants some feedback on his haiku poems. The timer is set to go off at 9:45. At that time, some of the children will want to share what they've been doing. I think I'll share what Krissa, Solomon, and I have been doing with quotation marks.

What can we do at home?

✎ Make a game of finding different forms of writing. How many different forms can you find in one day? in one week? in one car ride? During a single car ride, you might see billboards, flyers, brochures, signs, labels, license plates, magazines, books, bumper stickers, or campaign buttons.

✎ Ask your children about the time they spend writing in school. Do they write at least once a day?

✎ Are your children writing at school in different forms for different audiences and for different purposes?

Vary the writing your children do at home and make sure they are aware of writing in different forms for different audiences and for different purposes. Create a family newspaper that can be copied and sent out to grandparents, cousins, and friends. Ask your children to help you make grocery lists and schedules of chores. Let children design their own special thank-you notes. Publish a magazine that chronicles family activities for the year to give as a holiday gift. Any parent or grandparent would be proud to wear a specially-designed button (hot glue or sew a safety pin to the back of a disc-shaped paper). Transcribe very young children's dictated stories, or have older schoolchildren write their own stories, and then bind the stories with special paper to make a one-of-a-kind book.

Collect the different kinds of writing that you create or read, and then share them with your children. Help them see the differences as well as the reason for the differences: A manual you read before you set the timer on the VCR is different from the letter you write to a Congressperson or to a family member; a book you read aloud to your children is different from the newspaper article about a natural disaster or from a recipe for bread.

Encourage your children to keep a daily journal. Just a line or two each day is enough. Younger children will love adding illustrations.

Keep a family journal that every family member can write in and that all family members can read. Each day, record what the family has done. If you can remember family stories you heard when you were growing up, add them to this growing written record of your family's history. The entries in the family journal do not have to be in any particular order. Yesterday's entry might be the picnic you had in the pocket park down the street. Today's entry might be the funny name your son has for green beans. Tomorrow's entry might be a story your mother told you about her first bicycle. Add a combination of hand-drawn illustrations and photographs to the journal.

This list of suggested activites is short, and is designed only as a springboard for your own ideas. Begin with an activity you can do easily and comfortably with your children. Then add those activities that work especially well for you and your children.

Freewriting

Freewriting is a classroom practice that is used to "free up" writers' thought processes. Freewriting is usually nonstop writing within a set period of time. The writing that is produced in that time is not evaluated in terms of spelling, punctuation, or any other traditional rubric (set of standards) for writing. In fact, it is generally not read by anyone except the writer and is not even considered a first draft of any sort. It is, simply, unconditionally accepted words on paper. So why freewrite? Here are three reasons. First, having a quantity of writing is important to young authors. If they have written only 50 lines, then they are loath to part with any of them during revisions, regardless of how poor or glorious those lines might be. If, on the other hand, they have written several hundred or several thousand lines, then they are more likely to delete or alter lines. Second, freewriting can pull young writers away from focusing on single words or short phrases and back to larger ideas. Third, freewriting can help set free lots of new ideas for writing.

Freewriting, then, literally frees the writer to write whatever comes quickly and unbidden in a set period of time, and the products of this writing are free from judgment. Freewriting often frees thoughts and text that might otherwise be inhibited if the writer knows that the writing will be shared or evaluated.

What can freewriting look like?

Denise sits at the kitchen table with her fifth-grade daughter, Lauren, and her first-grade son, Cameron. Each child has a blank piece of paper and is holding a pencil in the air. Denise is holding a small black timer and gives last-minute instructions. "Now remember," she says, "just write. Don't worry about spelling or punctuation or if the ideas go together. Just write anything that comes to your mind and keep writing for ten minutes. Go!" All three pencils hit the papers at the same time, and the kitchen is filled with the scritch, scritch, scritch of ideas becoming visible on paper.

What can we do at home?

Sit down with your children and freewrite at the same time. Begin with setting the timer for a short period of time and then, as you all become more comfortable with the idea of freewriting, increase the amount of time that you freewrite. Try different shapes and colors of paper, and try some unusual pens or pencils.

After you have done some freewriting, begin by sharing aloud a word, a phrase, or an idea that you wrote during the freewriting. Invite your children to share a word, a phrase, or an idea. If they don't share at first, that's okay. Don't share the papers, because the focus might turn to correctness of spelling, punctuation, and handwriting rather than the writing or ideas that were freed.

This list of suggested activities is short, and is designed only as a springboard for your own ideas. Begin with an activity you can do easily and comfortably with your children. Then add those activities that work especially well for you and your children.

Process Writing

The idea of **process writing** in the classroom is very much like the idea of teaching people to swim by getting them in the water. There is much to learn about the history of swimming, and books have been written about the various theories of learning strokes and breathing techniques. But there is no substitute for getting into the water and practicing those strokes and breathing. Similarly, there is much to learn about the conventions of writing, and books have been written about the various forms and techniques of writing. But there is no substitute for putting pen to paper and practicing those forms and techniques of writing.

There are many different forms of writing that children can apply in their daily lives: lists, notes, letters, and requests, for example. Children become competent and confident with these forms when they use them often. Within the context of the classroom, they can be encouraged to attempt a wide range of forms, for a wide range of audiences, and for a wide range of purposes. Within the context of their writing, children can become aware of their growth and needs in writing. In other words, we learn writing by writing. By engaging in the process of writing, we become more accomplished writers.

Sometimes you will hear of "the writing process" described as a model of producing a piece of writing in which the steps of the process are linear: one step following another in a particular order. The linear model presented is usually (1) first draft, (2) revision, (3) publication. According to this model, a writer composed and wrote some thoughts (first draft); revised a least once for content changes and for corrections such as usage, spelling, and punctuation (revision); and then rewrote a final time with all corrections made and with a particular format (publication).

The linear model is obviously too simplistic a model to represent what truly goes on in a writer's world. Some writers consciously or unconsciously revise a great deal in their minds before they even put their thoughts down on paper, and so their first drafts are much more polished than others' first drafts. For example, my husband's first drafts are not very different from his last drafts because he thinks and rethinks many times before he sets pen to paper. In contrast, my first dozen drafts may range from lists, to outlines, to collections of phrases. Each draft will probably end up as a crumpled paper on the floor, and will look very little like my final draft.

For writers, some pieces may need no revision or just one revision. Other pieces may need multiple revisions. Some pieces of writing can be revised and rewritten after they have been published, and other pieces may never be published in any formal sense. Writers may have several pieces of writing in various stages of development that they are working on. In other words, a writer can enter any stage of the writing process at any time with any piece of writing. In a classroom setting, however, teachers may from time to time have children bring a piece through a process from first thoughts to publication so that the children are familiar with the various stages a piece of writing might be in.

Imagine illustrating and binding your own story and having it placed in the school media center for checkout, or having your letter to the editor published in the local newspaper. Imagine having several pieces in your writing folder that you could work on, depending on your motivation: a sequel to your last story, a poem about Mother's Day, a letter to the student council requesting a special ice cream sale, or an illustration for the narrative about your broken arm.

Just as the swimmer learns to swim by swimming and by experimenting and practicing a variety of strokes and breathing techniques, the writer learns to write by writing and by experimenting and practicing a variety of forms and techniques. With the swimmer, not every lap in a meet is for a ribbon, and the swimmer doesn't necessarily excel in every stroke. With the writer, not every piece is for publication, and the writer doesn't necessarily excel in every form of writing. Process writing can help provide the environment in which writers can experiment, practice, and excel.

What can we do at home?

Model your process writing to your children. When you write a letter, do you first make a list of points you want to write about? Is the first draft the final draft or do you rewrite it at least once?

Have a special drawer or decorated box where your children can keep pieces of writing in different stages. Tonight your son might start writing a story or your daughter might draw the illustrations for a book she's making. It might take two or three days to write a letter to Grandmom. Stock the drawer or box with special papers, pens, and pencils. To encourage revision, add highlighting pens, scissors, and glue or tape (to facilitate adding, deleting, cutting apart, and putting together in different ways).

✎   Encourage your children to take out a piece they've written before and do something different with it.

✎   Ask your children's teachers about opportunities for process writing during the school day. Is there class time for going back over pieces they have written and making them different? better?

This list of suggested activites is short, and is designed only as a springboard for your own ideas. Begin with an activity you can do easily and comfortably with your children. Then add those activities that work especially well for you and your children.

Invented Spelling

Invented spelling refers to any spelling of a word which is not its "correct" spelling as it is listed in a dictionary. Correctness in spelling can vary from country to country ("color" in the United States, "colour" in the United Kingdom), can evolve through time (colonial "shoppe" to contemporary "shop"), and can even include multiple correct forms ("aesthetic" and "esthetic"). In preschool and school settings, however, the term invented spelling usually refers to attempts by young writers to compensate for their not knowing the correct spelling of a word by substituting a letter or combination of letters. A young writer could invent the spelling "jraf" for the correct spelling, "giraffe." You or I might invent the spelling "tarmeggan" for the correct spelling, "ptarmigan."

When my children first began writing, there were combinations of letters and other symbols that only they could decipher. But they were writers. They understood that marks on a page could have meaning for someone, and they understood that they could control those marks and communicate with other people. As they learned more and more of the letter-sound relationships, their writing became easier for me to decipher. For example, if Kip wrote, "I kn go thr," I knew that he had written a form of "I can go there," because I had enough letter sounds to help me come up with the same sentence.

Context of the words (the surrounding words) helps us figure out invented spelling or the words that were not spelled correctly. Lack of context makes figuring out invented spelling much more difficult. If a child writes the single word "bot," we might not know for sure if the child means "boat" or "bought," but if the child writes "I salde mi bot," or "I bot a buk at th str," then the context will help us figure out whether the child means "boat" or "bought."

Why is invented spelling important? It is a transitional step that allows the writer to keep the focus away from correctness in spelling at a point in the writing process when it's better to write, write, write. Invented spelling allows beginning writers to write and to focus on the ideas, not simply be limited to the letters and sounds that they know. When my preschool daughter slipped a heart-shaped note into my pocket with the message, "yor grat," I would not have corrected her spelling. She was not concerned with the correctness of spelling in her messages to me, and so I received many, many messages in those preschool years. She took notes on "erthkwaks" and wrote to her brother in the Navy about the "klab in the bak yrd" they were building. The television would be turned off and have this note taped on it: "kleenuptim." Libby is in sixth grade now and is still a frequent and confident writer. She is also, incidentally, a very good speller.

Invented spelling allows developing writers to write, and not simply be limited to vocabulary they can spell correctly. First graders may want to write about "nyts and casuls and dragnz" even though they can't spell them correctly. Fifth graders might want to describe "the afects of aer preshr and wing desine on flite" before they can spell them correctly.

Invented spelling allows adult writers to write more than what they can spell, knowing they can use a dictionary or spellchecker when they're ready for that phase of the writing process. By my computer, I have taped up a list of words that includes "accommodation, occurrence, and occasion," but I don't refer to that list until my ideas are down and I'm ready to share the writing with someone else.

Invented spelling is a transition, an opportunity for writers of any age to let the ideas flow, unhindered by a premature concern for spelling, not limited by the restraint to write only about those things they can spell correctly. Correctness of spelling is important later in the writing process, and a concern for correctness in spelling comes naturally to writers of any age who are conscious of purpose and audience.

What can invented spelling look like?

My preschooler, Libby, was fond of taping messages and lists all around the house. "Gong to the mole" let me know she was excited about going to the mall. When I read that I was "slim from kor of teh erth," I thought at first she was angry, but she was just teasing me and proud that she knew about slime from the core of the earth.

What can we do at home?

✎ Look for patterns in your children's writing. If your fifth grader consistently writes "whent" instead of "went," then focus on just that one word for a few days.

✎ If you know your children will be writing about a particular topic, sit down together and make a list (word bank) of words they might use. A word bank for thank-you notes might include "thank you, appreciate, grateful, grandmother, money, buy, store, mall, birthday." Keep a file of word banks and add to them.

✎ Find out what your children's teachers are doing with spelling in the classroom. Is there a weekly list? Is there a pattern to the list? Are there dictation sentences each week? Does the teacher make individualized lists from each child's problem words?

✎ Discuss with your children the kinds of situations when correct spelling is very important (business letter, résumé, flier, poster, letter to the editor, for example) and when it is not.

✎ Be a "living dictionary" for your children, editing their writing for correctness in spelling and selecting one misspelled word as a focus word for a week or two.

This list of suggested activites is short, and is designed only as a springboard for your own ideas. Begin with an activity you can do easily and comfortably with your children. Then add those activities that work especially well for you and your children.

Poetry

Poetry is more than words that rhyme. It is a piece of writing that is special because of its beauty or power in language or expression. Poetry is also a form of writing that provides unique language opportunities both at home and in the classroom. Some of the characteristics of poetry that contribute particularly to its beauty are similes and metaphors, onomatopoeia, alliteration, and hyperbole. There are many more characteristics, and each one provides a special opportunity in school or at home.

Poetry forms can range from predictable old favorites such as "Roses are red..."; to formula poems such as lyrics, sonnets, and haiku; to free verse; to concrete poems in which the words on a page form a particular shape.

Poems are condensed pieces of writing. That is, the poet is presenting a great deal to the reader in a piece of writing smaller than a novel or short story. Each single word is important, and so young writers learn to look very critically at each word they are using. As a classroom teacher, I find that poetry is a great way to engage the writers in multiple revisions, because the revising and rewriting of poetry usually involves working with only one page of text.

Poems can be read aloud or silently, but they don't need to be picked apart and analyzed to death. Poet Lee Bennett Hopkins wrote, "Read poetry for the love and the fun of it—then leave it alone!" (*Speaking of Poets: Interviews with Poets Who Write for Children and Young Adults,* by Jeffrey S. Copeland; NCTE: 1993, p. 80.)

Poetry, whether it is composed or consumed, is a wonderful way to revel in our language. Children of all ages are eager revelers, from their first reciting of "Twinkle, Twinkle, Little Star," to the first reciting of their own poetry.

What can poetry writing look like?

Kacie, a fourth grader, was a prolific writer. Her stories averaged eight typewritten pages, and her classmates always looked forward to hearing her read them because they were really good. She was an avid reader too. This morning, she had been curled up in the corner reading a book about the Titanic. Tears rolled down her cheeks long before she closed the book, and they continued to fall as she pulled out her journal and began to write. She finished writing after lunch and came up for a conference with me. The poem was a powerful piece about the tragedy aboard the Titanic. I thought it was one of the best pieces she had ever written. She agreed, but worried about the length. Jono piped up from the other side of the table. "Why don't you write it like Byrd Baylor does her poems?" He was referring to Baylor's free verse poetry. Together, Jono and Kacie worked the rest of the afternoon on what became the Titanic poem, weighing each word to decide whether it should stand alone or with other words. The result was a free verse poem that won first place in the district's poetry contest.

What can we do at home?

Read lots of poetry to your children. Read a wide range of poetry from nursery rhymes to classics such as "Rime of the Ancient Mariner" (Coleridge) or "The Raven" (Poe). Even preschoolers can delight in the rhythm and rhyme of some of the classics.

Play a rhyming game where one person says a word and everyone else must take turns saying a word that rhymes with it. Or, as a variation of the game, have one person say a word and everyone else find words on billboards and signs that rhyme with the word. This is a great activity to do in the car.

Select some favorite poems for everyone to memorize and recite with lots of expression.

Recite the first line of a pattern rhyme and have everyone else compose a rhyming ending. For example, if you recite, "Roses are red, violets are purple," someone else might complete with "If I eat bread, I'll have to burple."

Play an alliteration game. The first person begins a sentence and everyone else must continue the sentence using the same beginning letter or sound. For example, if you begin,

"California condors," then the next person could say, "California condors can't," and the next person could say, "California condors can't count," and the next person could say, "California condors can't count cars."

Play a simile game. The first person begins by saying a phrase such as, "I'm as thirsty as…" The others must complete the simile. Sample completions could be "I'm as thirsty as an 18-wheeler on empty." or "I'm as thirsty as an Arizona desert."

Play a similar game with metaphors. The first person will give a situation such as "I'm hungry." The next person will provide a metaphor such as, "I'm a fireplace with no wood."

Take a favorite fairy tale, short story, newspaper article, or story that one of the children has written and turn it into a free-verse poem: free verse doesn't have to rhyme, or have each line begin with an upper-case letter, or have any particular number of syllables or words on each line.

Create concrete poems. Pick a shape and write a poem in that shape. For example, during football season, you could write poems about football in the shape of a football, a helmet, or goal posts. Winter poems could be written in the shape of pine trees, snowflakes, mittens, or sleds.

This list of suggested activites is short, and is designed only as a springboard for your own ideas. Begin with an activity you can do easily and comfortably with your children. Then add those activities that work especially well for you and your children.

ACROSS THE DISCIPLINES

Disciplines in school curricula serve to separate the areas that children study into general categories such as reading, writing, science, social studies, math, music, and so on. Although separating what children learn into categories may be convenient for discussing the individual disciplines, it is not the reality of any particular learning event. Let's look at writing as a discipline. When we support writing as a discipline, it's because we want our children to be able to write well. They may be writing about science, math, or social studies. They may be writing to understand better what they're thinking and learning and observing in science, math, or social studies. They may be writing to become more effective writers, all the while reading and rereading what they have written, perhaps even discussing it or dramatizing it. The pencil may be making marks on the paper, but each act of writing, each writing event, is connected to many other events and experiences at the same time.

Let's put across the disciplines in the context of a classroom. If second graders are learning about frogs in science, they (the children, not the frogs) might

- record their observations in a science log by writing and drawing.
- read to find out more so that they can form some hypotheses.
- discuss their findings with others in the class.
- dramatize the life cycle with puppets, music, and dance.
- create a graph or chart to illustrate the growth pattern.
- read or write fiction books about frogs.
- write a big picture book for younger children on the topic of frogs.
- label on a world map where different species of frogs live.

All of these activities are in the area of science, but they are also language arts, math, social studies, and music. Imagine how rich the children's understanding of frogs will be if they participate in those activities!

In this section, I've included **literature across the disciplines, integrated language arts,** and **thematic units** because they are ways of arranging the curriculum and the school day that provide opportunities for children to learn the depth and breadth of a topic, they provide opportunities for children to learn in unique and varied ways, and they provide opportunities for children to express and share their learning in a wealth of ways.

I've also included **family literacy** in this section for several reasons. The home is the first place where literacy learning takes place; children learn to value literacy and learning from their family's modeling; and the home is a natural place where literacy and learning cut across all of life's events and experiences and are not broken down to fit into neat curriculum charts or time schedules.

Literature across Disciplines

Thanks to the wonderful proliferation of children's books the past few years, library shelves are filled with fiction as well as nonfiction books that illustrate or support concepts that can be categorized as math, science, social studies, or any of the other separate disciplines. And the books illustrate or support those concepts in ways that interest children—even entertain them—and allow them to make connections to other areas of interest, information, or their own personal lives.

The three books that the fifth graders read in the following vignette were dramatic illustrations of different perspectives during the Civil War. Those three books were special because they underscored the power of reading and writing at the same time that they put important historical events in the memorable context of story.

The three books in the vignette could constitute what is termed a "text set." A text set is a collection of books that have a common author, genre (fantasy, mystery, biography, etc.), theme, or other common thread that either the teacher or the children could identify. With all three of those books, language, as well as the telling of the story of the Civil War, is a common thread.

As a parent, you could make text sets with counting books, books about farm animals, or a set of tall tales. You could also bring the power of story to whatever concept or idea you're teaching your children by reading some of your own family letters and diaries, or by telling stories of your own experience and family that reinforce something you're teaching your children. The power of story and the label of literature are not confined to trade books alone. Unpublished stories share that same power and have the right to be called literature.

What can literature across the disciplines look like?

The fifth-grade class was studying the Civil War. In January, Laura and Joleen had read *Nettie's Trip South* to their reading buddies and wanted to share it with the rest of the fifth graders. Laura and Joleen took turns reading the book in the role of Nettie, traveling south and encountering slavery for the first time. When they were finished, their classmates responded that they had really felt the impact of slavery on a young girl. Several of the boys wanted to do a dramatic reading too, so they chose *The Boys' War*, a book based on diary entries and letters from boys in the Civil War. After their production, Lacey said, "Nettie and Boys' War were really about writing, weren't they?" "I've got one that's really about reading," said Janeeta. "It's *Night John* by Gary Paulsen." She went on to explain that Night John was an escaped slave who returns, risking dismemberment, so that he can teach other slaves to read. The fifth graders decided that they'd like to have the story as a readaloud.

Tara Kesler, age 8

What can we do at home?

✏️ Check with your children's teachers to find out what concepts they will be studying in class. Ask the teachers if they have any suggestions for literature that would support or illustrate those concepts. Go to the local library and ask the librarian for suggestions of appropriate literature.

✏️ Make a text set. Select several books that you feel have a common theme or thread. Ask your children to identify that common theme or thread.

✏️ Ask your children to make literature sets and then think of special ways to package them. For example, you could place four books that have to do with bedtime in a pretty pillowcase. Place six books about birthdays in a gift bag. Cover a shoe box with numerals and place five books inside that have to do with math.

✏️ Think of some of your favorite books or movies, from childhood to adulthood. Did any of them help reinforce something you were learning about? If one is at an appropriate age level for your children, share it and share how it was special for you. The movies *Johnny Tremain* and *How the West Was Won* helped make moments in history memorable for me.

This list of suggested activites is short, and is designed only as a springboard for your own ideas. Begin with an activity you can do easily and comfortably with your children. Then add those activities that work especially well for you and your children.

Integrated Language Arts

It's difficult to imagine performing any one of the language arts (traditionally listed as reading, writing, speaking, and listening) without any interaction with one of the other language arts. Some schools, however, have scheduled children for separate instruction in different aspects of the language arts. A schedule that supports separate instruction may have spelling for 20 minutes, handwriting for 15 minutes, reading for 45 minutes, and grammar and usage for 20 minutes. Curriculum demands on today's school schedules make it harder and harder to keep those aspects of language arts separate.

In an integrated language arts program, the children (individually, in small groups, or as a total class) focus on different aspects of the language arts in the context of what they are doing at the time. For example, if a teacher notices that several of the children are trying to use quotation marks in their writing, the teacher could bring those children together for a short seminar on quotation marks, using illustrations from their literature, and having the children dramatize by reading aloud only the text that is in quotation marks. In another example, rather than teach similes and metaphors and follow up with practice worksheets, the teacher could use the literature the children are already reading to locate samples of similes and metaphors, and then encourage the children to use similes and metaphors through poetry writing.

What can integrated language arts look like?

The school's student council had selected a different theme for each month of the school year. November's theme was respect. The first graders were particularly excited about this theme because they had been discussing it a lot in their literature studies: respect for each other, for families, for nature. At first, they wanted to make some posters to place around their classroom to remind each other to focus on respect during the month. The posters were so good, though, that the students wanted to share them with the rest of the school. They wrote a letter to the principal, asking to put their posters around the school. She agreed that it was a great idea and suggested that they also go around to each classroom to announce the posters. When the children divided up the classrooms to visit, they decided that they would also perform a short skit to illustrate how their schoolmates could demonstrate respect. Within two days, they took their shows on the road. Both the skits and the posters were a big hit.

What can we do at home?

✎   Write down a list of questions you have for your children's teachers. How are the language arts taught in the class? Are the teachers restricted by chunks of time that must be devoted to separate, isolated aspects of language arts? Are the language arts integrated so that the children are engaged in literacy events that involve more than one or all of the language arts?

✎   What sorts of assessments or tests are required of your children? In spelling, for example, do they have lists of spelling words they must learn for a weekly test? Are the spelling words connected in any way to the children's writing? to the child r s reading? to what the children are studying?

✎   Try some variations with family reading. Take turns dramatizing dialogue from a story. Read aloud instead of silently.

✎   If you're reading a chapter book together, begin a family response journal. A family response journal can be several pieces of paper that are simply stapled together with an illustration of the book on the cover sheet, or it can be a specially bound book of blank pages. One family member begins by responding in the family response journal to what was read. The next family member takes the journal and can respond to the first family member's writing or can write a completely independent response. The journal is circulated until every family member has had the opportunity to participate in the journal.

This list of suggested activites is short, and is designed only as a springboard for your own ideas. Begin with an activity you can do easily and comfortably with your children. Then add those activities that work especially well for you and your children.

Thematic Units

With thematic units, teachers try to tie the curriculum together with a common thread or overarching theme. The common threads or themes seem to help children grasp a number of ideas, and they provide more opportunities for children to apply their understanding of those themes in a variety of disciplines.

For example, the fifth-grade curriculum in my school includes chemistry and a study of pre-Columbian American history, so our overarching theme for the first nine weeks of school is "beginnings." Under the theme of "beginnings," students are involved with lots of activities having to do with the beginning of the school year; the beginnings of human history in the Americas with the migration of Asians over Beringia to Alaska; chemistry as the beginning or building blocks of life; and literature that focuses on characters struggling with beginnings.

Thematic units can be authentic or they can lapse into being contrived. For example, if a third-grade class is studying bears, writing a story problem that reads, "Ten bears were walking in the clearing. Six of the bears walked into the woods. How many bears were left?" is contrived because it's not particularly about bears except that it does use bears in the text. The bears in the story problem could just as easily have been replaced by rabbits or marauding Visigoths. A more authentic use of the theme might be to pose a problem about bear overpopulation in a particular region and have the children pose solutions, applying what knowledge they have about bear habitats and amounts of food consumed.

There is no prescribed length of time for engaging children in a thematic unit. Depending on the range of the topic and the interest level of the children, a thematic unit might last a couple of days or an entire school year. What characterizes a thematic unit is that there is an overarching theme that ties together many or all aspects of the curriculum: math, science, social studies, reading, writing, and so on.

What can thematic units look like?

Jill came home from first grade all excited. "Rakesh's arm got broke and we're gonna study dinosaurs!" Feeling as though he had somehow missed a connection, Jill's father asked, "What does Rakesh's arm have to do with dinosaurs?" What he found out was that when Rakesh came to school this morning, he was waving a new, blue cast on his right forearm. Rakesh's arm was broken when he fell off his bicycle late yesterday afternoon. When he showed his classmates the X-ray today, one of them exclaimed, "That looks like a dinosaur bone!" "No it doesn't," countered another child. "Yes it does 'cause I seen lots at the museum," another first grader piped up. There was a lively discussion during which the children challenged each other about what they knew and didn't know about dinosaurs. Four weeks later, Jill's father went to her first grade classroom to see a play about dinosaurs. The children shared books they had written, charts and posters they had drawn, a map they had drawn indicating where the Jurassic critters had roamed, a mathematical projection of how long it would take Rakesh's arm to fossilize, and many more projects.

What can we do at home?

✐   Ask your children's teachers if the curriculum is set up in thematic units. Themes might determine how the class looks at material learned in a grading quarter. Themes might emerge from the children's experiences or events. Ask how you can help support the themes.

✐   Think up themes that are easy and fun at home. If a child expresses an interest in dogs, for example, you can find fiction and nonfiction literature about dogs; visit a dog kennel or the city pound; rent a movie about dogs; look up the countries of origin for different kinds of dogs; find out more about dog training schools; learn some fun songs about dogs.

✐   If you are going on a family trip, involve all the family members in researching the route and the destination. Calculate the number of miles to drive or travel each day; calculate a budget for the trip; plan meals or food; plot out the route on a large map; put together activity bags that include books and journals; read books about places along the route and the destination; read about other fictional and nonfictional trips.

This list of suggested activites is short, and is designed only as a springboard for your own ideas. Begin with an activity you can do easily and comfortably with your children. Then add those activities that work especially well for you and your children.

Family Literacy

Family literacy is a concept that acknowledges a school child's family and household members in their critical roles as literacy supporters and nurturers. Family literacy is a concept that includes the home environment and home activities as contributors to a child's literacy.

Family literacy can focus primarily on the school child, or it can focus on a family group which includes a school child. When the focus is beyond the child, then it is termed intergenerational and can be limited to the parents' generation, or can include grandparents or even great grandparents.

There are many ways that a family member can support and nurture literacy in the home. For example, when there are books and magazines in the home that are either part of the family library or checked out from the local library, then family members are more likely to model reading or read aloud to the children. A parent or grandparent who is struggling with literacy and learning to read or write can provide the inspiration and motivation for a school child.

Sometimes, family members are literate in another language but are just acquiring literacy in English. The children can be a vital part of that English literacy acquisition by supporting the family members or by learning along with them.

Family literacy is not measured by engagement with printed text alone. The oral tradition is a very powerful way in which family members pass on family history and stories, and build a foundation of positive and frequent communication. Family literacy cannot be measured solely by school standards. There are many contexts and life situations which demand various types and degrees of literacy.

Whether the term family literacy is used in a child-centered or family-centered sense, every engagement of families in acts of literacy such as reading, writing, storytelling, talking, and listening contributes to the literacy of a child.

What can family literacy look like?

In my closet, there's a special box, cardboard edges split with age, held together with ribbon that tears every time I untie it. Inside are my father's letters, written to me almost 50 years ago. They are faded with age, but they paint a picture of family literacy. In April 1951, I was six years old. My father drove from Lima (Peru) to Ica, and I had written him a letter. This was his reply to me later that day: "Dear Jane, Thank you so much for your very loving letter you gave me when I left Lima. When I got to Ica I was very tired. Then I remember you said to read your letter after I got to Ica. I got it and read it and was very very happy. I am going to keep this letter and read it often while I am away from home. Lots of love from Daddy."

What can we do at home?

Let your children see you reading for pleasure. Share some vocabulary or great phrases, a character, or even part of the story line with them. See if there are any similarities with books that your children are reading.

Talk to your children about how your parents read to you or told you stories.

Let your children see you write for pleasure. Send family letters to relatives or friends. Let everyone in the family contribute a part or an illustration.

When you're riding in the car, tell your children a story about when you were little, or tell them a story about something that happened at work that day. Leave off the ending and let them provide an ending.

Have your children select three things they want included in a story. Make up a story that includes those three things. For example, the selections might be a princess, a race car, and an ice cream cone. The children will love helping you find clever ways to include their three things in the story.

When you pass a rock formation, landmark, building, or street sign, take turns with the children thinking up a legend behind the name or creation of the item. Even though you might all be familiar with the actual background story, making one up is lots of fun. At night, you might think up legends for the face in the moon. Follow up these storytelling events with a trip to the library to find out legends from other countries or groups.

Try different ambiences for your readalouds or storytelling. If it's a scary story, for example, tell it in the dark or read it with flashlights. If it's a story about when one of your children was an infant, bring out an old toy and hold it as you tell the story.

Try themes in your family literacy events. This works naturally with holidays, but lots of different themes can be used any time. If your family has chosen popcorn as a theme, look through magazines for pictures of popcorn; make a collage of places where you might eat popcorn; find packaged foods in the grocery store that contain popcorn; list all the different kinds of popcorn available; pop some popcorn, with everyone helping to read the recipe; trade popcorn stories (when did you first string popcorn, or first eat it in the movie theater) and make a little book of those stories; select books (fiction and nonfiction) that have to do with popcorn and read them aloud.

Make a family book that is a collection of stories: favorites retold generation after generation or stories of family events (first visit by the tooth fairy). Any time that stories are recorded, younger children can dictate to an older family member.

✎   When you go on a trip, keep a family journal, writing down impressions and events, keeping postcards or illustrations, noting unusual names for places, or recording strange stories from different places.

✎   Keep a list on the refrigerator of foods that need to be bought at the grocery store. Have children help add to the list and, when you go shopping, have the children read the list, find the items, read packages for information, and check items off the list.

✎   Keep a little note pad or recycled pieces of paper next to the telephone. Use that area as a message center where family members can leave telephone messages or other notes to each other. You can even turn the message center into a little post office with little boxes or pockets for each family member.

✎   Keep a family calendar in a central place, such as the family message center. The best calendars for this are ones with large boxes for each day so that your children can enter their own special dates or draw pictures as reminders.

✎   If you watch the news on television, discuss the news with your children; compare the television or radio news to an article in the newspaper.

✎   When you watch a movie, talk about the characters, about how important the setting (time and place) were in the movie, about the sequence of events. Ask how the movie compares with a book and discuss an alternative you or the children might have written for the movie.

✎   Discuss television viewing with your children and then have your children use the television guide to make a daily chart of programs they will watch. Read the short summaries of plots and descriptions of programs.

Use whatever the children have watched on television to connect to books. Help the children find books that give more information about something that has interested them on television.

Members of older generations make wonderful readers for young children, and children also make wonderful readers for older listeners. Children can read their own writing, a favorite story, or magazines and newspapers. Two or more generations can collaborate on a story or book. Using special paper to write on or binding it makes the book even more special.

Have a bookmark-making party. Have each family member write his or her name on a piece of paper and list favorite topics or books. Place all the papers in a box and have each member draw a name and design a bookmark specially for that other family member.

This list of suggested activites is short, and is designed only as a springboard for your own ideas. Begin with an activity you can do easily and comfortably with your children. Then add those activities that work especially well for you and your children.

CONCLUSION

This book has presented several sets of concepts, illustrations of how those concepts can be played out in classrooms and homes, and a beginning list of suggested home activities to support a level and sophistication of literacy that should serve your children well in the 21st century.

Everything presented and represented in this book, however, is little more than hope and vision without the most important piece: you. As a parent, a teacher, and a professional leader, I can tell you without question that the most important element in preparing your children for the 21st century is you. School days and school years vary in length, teachers and methods vary, the quality and quantity of materials and resources vary. But you and your caring are the constants in your children's lives. You are the ones at home who model attitudes toward the goals and purposes for learning which will lead to success in the 21st century.

The activities in this book don't require an investment of money. Find out what your local resources are and take full advantage of them: public and school libraries, thrift stores, secondhand book stores. Find out what your personal resources are and take full advantage of them: share your family stories and your work experiences, write, read, speak, and listen to your children.

The activities in this book do require an investment of time in frequent literacy events that are planned as well as serendipitous. Preparing your children for literacy in the 21st century might not happen if you plan a several-hours-long literacy event once a month; but it might happen if you sing a rhyme in the car on the way to the grocery store, read a story at bedtime, and smuggle a love note into a lunchbox a couple times a week.

The activities in this book are only a springboard. You know your children and yourself better than anyone else does. Use your children's strengths and favorites and your own strengths and favorites as a starting point.

This book represents a single moment in the evolution of literacy, a quick dip into the language arts stream to look at water that will be different with each dip. Keep dipping! Revel in the continually changing expressions and demands of literacy. Every day there are new books, new magazines, new ways of using print, film, radio, television, and computers.

This book represents an initial but grand dialogue that includes other parents, your children, classroom teachers, and the technological, social, and political world around you. Continue the dialogue each day with your children: continue to build bridges between your children's school experiences and their out-of-school experiences. Continue the dialogue with your children's teachers: find out all you can about what's going on in the classroom and why, and ask how you can be a part of it or support it even though you can't be physically in the classroom. Continue the dialogue with other parents: share what works and what doesn't work. Keep up with evolving definitions, methods, and materials. Children and learning are at the center of the missions and goals for professional education organizations such as the National Council of Teachers of English (800-369-6283), the National Parent Information Network (800-583-4135), and the National PTA (312-670-6782). You can continue the dialogue by contacting these organizations; reading their journals, books, or pamphlets; attending their conferences or workshops; accessing their World Wide Web sites, or acquiring video-tapes and audiotapes and other materials that are available through their catalogs.

We can't envision exactly what the literacy demands of the next century will be for our children. We can, however, envision preparing our children in such a way that they will welcome and exceed those demands; and we can envision that preparation coming about only with school and home working together for literacy in the 21st century.

About the Author

Janie Hydrick, Ph.D., has served the educational community in a wide variety of functions for 30 years. She has taught at all grade levels from first grade through adult education; currently she teaches fifth grade at Entz Elementary School in Mesa, Arizona. Hydrick served as the Western States Romper Room teacher from 1966 through 1969 (spying thousands of viewers daily in her magic mirror), and more recently has taught the educational uses of computers from kindergarten through the college level.

Professionally, she has served as President of the National Council of Teachers of English and as Chair of NCTE's Elementary Section. She currently serves as a Director on the National Board for Professional Teaching Standards and on the Curriculum Advisory Board for the Lightspan Partnership. In 1989, Hydrick received the Excellence in Language Arts Teaching Award from the Arizona English Teachers Association.

She is the mother of Kip, a freshman at Arizona State University, and Libby, a sixth grader at Aprende Middle School in Chandler, Arizona.